The Better, Faster,
CRISPIER-THAN-TAKEOUT
» AIR FRYER «
COOKBOOK

OVER 75 QUICK & EASY RESTAURANT RECIPES

ELLA SANDERS
BESTSELLING AUTHOR OF *THE SKINNY AIR FRYER COOKBOOK*

CASTLE POINT BOOKS
NEW YORK

www.castlepointbooks.com

The Castle Point Books trademark is owned by Castle Point Publishing, LLC.
Castle Point books are published and distributed by St. Martin's Publishing Group.

ISBN 978-1-250-33980-5 (trade paperback)
ISBN 978-1-250-33981-2 (ebook)

Design by Tara Long
Photography under license from Shutterstock.com

Our books may be purchased in bulk for promotional, educational, or business use.
Please contact your local bookseller or the Macmillan Corporate and Premium Sales
Department at 1-800-221-7945, extension 5442, or by email
at MacmillanSpecialMarkets@macmillan.com.

First Edition: 2024

10 9 8 7 6 5 4 3 2 1

CONTENTS

ENJOY RESTAURANT FLAVOR AT HOME

GET ALL THE DELIGHTFUL FLAVORS OF EATING OUT WITHOUT ANY OF THE HASSLE! Say goodbye to placing pesky orders and hoping they get it right, waiting hangrily for disappointing takeout that arrives cold and soggy, or regretting a calorie explosion. With the right recipe and the perfect tool, you can whip up the same mouthwatering dishes much healthier and crispier in your own kitchen. Your air fryer is the secret to achieving restaurant-quality taste, smart nutritional choices, and a celebration of good, fun food any night of the week.

An air fryer—the countertop appliance that cooks food by circulating hot air around your ingredients—is magic for anyone who craves the satisfying crunch of a perfectly fried piece of chicken or a pile of crispy fries topped with shaved Parmesan and truffle oil. Even better: a good air fryer lets you skip the fuss of those deep fryers that many restaurants rely upon—with great results, less fat, and easy cleanup!

In this cookbook, you'll find more than 75 delicious recipes to savor—without waiting in line at the counter for your order to be ready. You'll recognize familiar favorites like Classic Chicken & Waffles (page 90), Best Barbecue Sliders (page 65), and Jalapeño Poppers (page 10). But there are also some surprises to try, like the Korean tacos that offer a perfect East meets West fusion experience (page 59) or the Hawaiian burger that explodes with flavor thanks to the red onion and pineapple toppings (page 69).

And if you have a sweet tooth, your taste buds just might transport you to your favorite sweet stops when you try the amazing desserts in this collection. Air-Fried Oreos (page 124), All-American Apple Dumplings (page 116), and even a glazed doughnut (page 120) require just a few simple ingredients and a little time in the air fryer to re-create the tempting treats you love.

SECRETS TO AIR FRYER MAGIC

Air fryers can vary greatly in their size and features, but the basic idea is the same—all include a fan to circulate hot air around your food. If yours has a cooking basket with removable racks, it's just a matter of pressing a few buttons to release the basket and load in your ingredients.

In most recipes, you just need to spritz the food with a little oil before placing it in the air fryer (a welcome—and healthy—change from the days of deep-frying everything). You can use commercial sprays but having an oil spray bottle that you can refill yourself is particularly handy and cost-effective. Just a few pumps produce a fine mist that will help prevent sticking and ensure a nice crispy coating from the air fryer.

Another benefit of air fryers: Midway through the cooking time, you can pause to release the basket and give it a quick shake instead of painstakingly turning every piece of food that's cooking. Some air fryers even come with a baking pan for pizzas and desserts. If you don't have a baking pan especially for your air fryer, a glass, silicone, or oven-safe metal dish will work.

When it comes to timing and temperature, because the size of the basket can vary, for best results it's always a good idea to pay close attention to whatever you have in the air fryer and adjust your cooking time accordingly. Whether or not you'll need to preheat your air fryer depends on which model you have, so check the instructions that came with yours. In general, preheating isn't necessary. But when it is, it only takes about 3 minutes.

Whatever you're cooking up, your air fryer makes it easy to get restaurant-style flavor with fast results and less fat. So, turn on your air fryer and let the festivities begin!

KEEPING IT FUN

Despite the fact that an air fryer may be one of the most convenient, easy-to-use appliances in your kitchen, remember that they are also powerful machines, so make sure to follow your manufacturer's safety recommendations carefully. Keep the following in mind:

- **Air fryers get extremely hot**—especially if you've added oil or steaming liquid to the pan. While your food cooks, liquids will accumulate in the cooking chamber, so always use caution when removing the basket. After the cooking cycle is complete, the basket will be very hot. So after removing it, make sure you place it only on heatproof surfaces.

- **During the cooking cycle, hot air or steam is released through the air outlets.** Be sure to keep your hands and face away from them. Don't place anything on top of the appliance during operation, and don't cover the air inlets or outlets.

- **Use a meat thermometer.** While the recipes in this collection offer visual cues to know what your food should look like when it's done, the only way to know for sure whether meats are cooked to a safe temperature is to rely on a meat thermometer.

STARTERS, SNACKS, AND SIDES

JALAPEÑO POPPERS 10

BUFFALO CAULIFLOWER BITES 13

AIR-FRIED PICKLES
WITH SPICY DIPPING SAUCE 14

IRRESISTIBLE
ROASTED CHICKPEAS 15

MEDITERRANEAN
SWEET POTATO FRIES 17

CRISPY GREEN BEANS 18

SPICY PUMPKIN FRIES 20

PARMESAN TRUFFLE FRIES 21

CLASSIC POUTINE 22

SOUTHWESTERN EGG ROLLS 25

VEGETABLE SAMOSAS 26

GRUYÈRE ARANCINI 28

AIR-FRIED RAVIOLI
WITH MARINARA 29

GOLDEN MAC & CHEESE BITES 30

JALAPEÑO POPPERS

MAKES
4 SERVINGS

PREP
10 MINUTES

TOTAL
20 MINUTES

12 jalapeño peppers

1 cup shredded
Monterey Jack cheese

4 ounces cream
cheese, softened

2 tablespoons mayonnaise

½ teaspoon salt, divided

½ teaspoon smoked
paprika, divided

½ teaspoon garlic
powder, divided

½ cup panko breadcrumbs

1 tablespoon olive oil

Ranch dressing, for
serving (optional)

Turn up the heat at home! These zesty starters owe a hint of smoky flavor to the paprika. And of course, everything is better with ranch dressing, so feel free to serve it on the side. Remember to be careful when handling the peppers—wear gloves and wash your hands thoroughly—so you don't get burned before the flavorful festivities even begin.

1. Preheat the air fryer to 380°F.

2. Cut the jalapeño peppers in half lengthwise. Use a spoon to scrape out and discard the seeds and ribs from the peppers. Set the halved peppers aside.

3. In a medium bowl, stir together the cheese, cream cheese, mayonnaise, and ¼ teaspoon each of salt, paprika, and garlic powder.

4. In a small bowl, stir together the breadcrumbs, olive oil, and the remaining ¼ teaspoon each of salt, paprika, and garlic powder.

5. Fill each pepper half with the cheese mixture, then sprinkle the tops of the peppers evenly with the breadcrumb mixture. Spritz generously with olive oil.

6. Working in batches if necessary, transfer the stuffed peppers to the air fryer basket. Air fry for 5 to 7 minutes, until the tops are brown and the cheese mixture is melted.

7. Serve the jalapeño poppers with ranch dressing on the side (if using).

→ · BUFFALO · ←
CAULIFLOWER BITES

⟩ MAKES ⟨
4 SERVINGS

⟩ PREP ⟨
15 MINUTES

⟩ TOTAL ⟨
25 MINUTES

1 cup all-purpose flour

1 tablespoon cornstarch

1 teaspoon salt

½ teaspoon freshly
ground black pepper

½ teaspoon garlic powder

½ teaspoon smoked paprika

1 cup buttermilk

1 head cauliflower, cut
into bite-size pieces

½ cup hot sauce

2 tablespoons butter, melted

2 tablespoons chopped
fresh cilantro

No need to drive around town looking for apps to please everyone. This veggie version of a fried favorite will earn high ratings across the board—even from family and friends who don't usually go the vegetarian route! It's all in the seasoned breading and sauce that coat the tender cauliflower bites. You'll get a perfect crisp on the outside in no time in your air fryer.

· ◆ ·

1. Preheat the air fryer to 400°F.

2. In a large bowl, stir together the flour, cornstarch, salt, pepper, garlic powder, and paprika. Place the buttermilk in another large bowl.

3. Working a few pieces at a time, dip the cauliflower into the flour mixture, then the buttermilk, and finally back into the flour mixture. Toss until the pieces are evenly coated, tapping gently to remove excess flour. Arrange the cauliflower in a single layer in the air fryer basket. Spritz with olive oil.

4. Working in batches if necessary, air fry for 7 minutes, pausing to shake the basket halfway through the cooking time.

5. While the cauliflower is in the air fryer, in another large bowl, whisk together the hot sauce and butter until smooth. When the cauliflower is browned and tender, transfer to the bowl and toss with the hot sauce mixture.

6. Top with the cilantro and serve with extra sauce on the side, if desired.

AIR-FRIED PICKLES
→ WITH SPICY DIPPING SAUCE ←

MAKES
4 SERVINGS

PREP
15 MINUTES

TOTAL
25 MINUTES

2 cups dill pickle slices

½ cup all-purpose flour

1 large egg

1 tablespoon water

½ cup panko breadcrumbs

¼ cup grated
Parmesan cheese

⅓ cup mayonnaise

2 tablespoons sriracha

There is just something about pickles that is so satisfying after a trip through your air fryer. An ordinary relish becomes an app that can stand on its own. Crunchy and tangy, this is a recipe to save for your next casual get-together with friends or as an easy starter for a Southern-style barbecue. Don't skip patting the pickles dry before coating—that step is key to making the breading stick!

. . . . ◆ . . . .

1. Preheat the air fryer to 400°F.

2. Lay the pickles on a paper towel and pat dry. In a shallow bowl, add the flour. In a second shallow bowl, add the egg and whisk with the water. In a third shallow bowl, add the breadcrumbs and cheese and stir until thoroughly combined.

3. Dip each pickle in the flour, then in the egg mixture, and lastly in the breadcrumb mixture.

4. Working in batches if necessary, arrange the pickles in a single layer in the air fryer basket and spritz with olive oil. Air fry for 8 to 10 minutes, pausing halfway through the cooking time to flip the pickles, until golden brown.

5. While the pickles cook, in a small bowl, combine the mayonnaise and sriracha. Stir until thoroughly combined.

6. Serve the pickles with the dipping sauce on the side.

→·IRRESISTIBLE·←
ROASTED CHICKPEAS

MAKES
4 SERVINGS

PREP
5 MINUTES

TOTAL
25 MINUTES

1 (19-ounce) can chickpeas, drained and rinsed

1 tablespoon olive oil

½ teaspoon smoked paprika

¼ teaspoon cayenne (optional)

¼ teaspoon garlic powder

¼ teaspoon onion powder

¼ teaspoon salt

These air-fried chickpeas loaded with spices make a super snack on their own, but they're also a great addition to salads or loaded into wrap sandwiches for a notable pop of flavor. The air fryer renders chickpeas crunchy and positively addictive. If chickpeas aren't your thing or you want to change it up, black-eyed peas make a good substitute.

· ◆ ·

1. Preheat the air fryer to 390°F.

2. In a large bowl, combine the chickpeas, olive oil, paprika, cayenne (if using), garlic powder, onion powder, and salt. Stir until the chickpeas are thoroughly coated with the oil and spices.

3. Transfer the chickpeas to the air fryer basket and air fry for 15 to 20 minutes, pausing to shake the basket every 5 minutes, until the chickpeas are browned and dry.

4. Let cool slightly before serving.

→ · MEDITERRANEAN · ←
SWEET POTATO FRIES

MAKES
2 SERVINGS

PREP
10 MINUTES

TOTAL
30 MINUTES

1 large sweet potato, peeled and cut into fries

1 tablespoon harissa

2 teaspoons olive oil

½ teaspoon kosher salt

¼ teaspoon freshly ground black pepper

¼ cup plain nonfat Greek yogurt

2 teaspoons fresh lemon juice

1 clove garlic, minced

¼ cup pomegranate seeds

2 tablespoons chopped fresh parsley or mint

You can have satisfying restaurant-style loaded fries anytime, right from your kitchen. Get ready for forkfuls of sweet, savory, and spicy—the perfect taste trifecta! The natural sweetness of the potatoes only intensifies in an air fryer. The tang of pomegranate seeds and the cooling yogurt sauce balance the kick of the harissa, a chili paste common in Tunisian cuisine.

· ◆ ·

1. Preheat the air fryer to 400°F.

2. In a medium bowl, combine the sweet potato, harissa, olive oil, salt, and pepper. Toss until the potatoes are thoroughly coated.

3. Transfer the sweet potato mixture to the air fryer basket. Air fry for 20 minutes, pausing halfway through the cooking time to shake the basket, until the potatoes are tender and browned.

4. Meanwhile, in a small bowl, stir together the yogurt, lemon juice, and garlic until thoroughly combined. Add salt and pepper to taste.

5. Serve the potatoes topped with the yogurt sauce, pomegranate seeds, and fresh herbs.

↬ · CRISPY · ↫
GREEN BEANS

↬ MAKES ↫
4 SERVINGS

↬ PREP ↫
15 MINUTES

↬ TOTAL ↫
25 MINUTES

½ cup all-purpose flour

½ teaspoon salt

2 large eggs

½ cup panko breadcrumbs

½ cup grated
Parmesan cheese

1 teaspoon garlic powder

1 pound green
beans, trimmed

Traditional French-fried potatoes aren't the only dip-worthy snack you can make in an air fryer. Why not mix it up and try green beans? You'll sneak in a green veggie even picky eaters will gobble up alone or alongside burgers. For this recipe, skip the preheat—the breaded beans handle better if you take them directly to the basket, but many air fryer models will turn off when you take the basket out. This defeats the purpose of preheating. In general, preheating is a good idea if you can load up the basket quickly.

· ·•◆•·· ·

1. In a large bowl, whisk together the flour and salt; set aside. In another large bowl, lightly beat the eggs; set aside. In a third large bowl, combine the breadcrumbs, cheese, and garlic powder and stir until thoroughly combined.

2. Working a few pieces at a time, dip the beans into the flour mixture, then in the eggs, and finally into the breadcrumb mixture. Toss until the pieces are evenly coated, tapping gently to remove excess crumbs. Arrange in a single layer in the bottom of an air fryer basket. Spritz with olive oil.

3. Working in batches if necessary, air fry at 400°F for 7 minutes, pausing to shake the basket halfway through the cooking time, until browned and crispy.

→ · SPICY · ←
PUMPKIN FRIES

MAKES
4 SERVINGS

PREP
15 MINUTES

TOTAL
30 MINUTES

1 medium sugar pumpkin or pie pumpkin

2 tablespoons olive oil

1 tablespoon barbecue seasoning rub

½ teaspoon salt

½ teaspoon garlic powder

½ teaspoon ground cinnamon

Here's yet another delicious way to enjoy pumpkin and spice together! This recipe takes a barbecue twist, but feel free to experiment with spice flavors. Whatever you choose, pumpkin fries cook up sweet and tender on the inside and crispy on the outside in minutes (and mess-free!) in your air fryer.

1. Preheat the air fryer to 390°F.

2. Using a sharp knife, cut the pumpkin in half. Scoop out the seeds and pulp. Cut half of the pumpkin into thin planks about the size of a French fry. Trim any pieces that have thick skin. Cover and refrigerate the remaining pumpkin half for another recipe.

3. In a large bowl, toss the pumpkin slices with the olive oil and sprinkle with the barbecue seasoning, salt, garlic powder, and cinnamon. Toss gently until the fries are thoroughly coated with the oil and seasonings.

4. Working in batches if necessary, arrange the fries in a single layer in the air fryer basket. Air fry for 12 to 15 minutes, pausing to shake the basket halfway through the cooking time, until the fries are browned and fork tender.

→ PARMESAN ←
TRUFFLE FRIES

MAKES
2 SERVINGS

PREP
15 MINUTES

TOTAL
35 MINUTES

2 russet potatoes

1 tablespoon olive oil

1 teaspoon salt

½ teaspoon freshly
ground black pepper

½ cup freshly grated
Parmigiano-Reggiano cheese

1 tablespoon chopped
fresh rosemary

1 teaspoon ground
truffle seasoning

1 tablespoon truffle oil
(optional)

These decadent gastro-pub favorites are perfect for
re-creating in your air fryer. Don't bother peeling the
potatoes—the skin adds both texture and flavor. Truffle
seasoning, a ground powder made largely from dried
truffles, is widely available online and in gourmet markets.
If you have a bottle of truffle oil tucked away in your
pantry, add another layer of fabulousness to these
unforgettable fries.

· ◆ ·

1. Preheat the air fryer to 400°F.

2. Cut the potatoes into French fry–size pieces (keep the
skin on for extra flavor).

3. In a large bowl, toss the potatoes, olive oil, salt, and
pepper until the potatoes are thoroughly coated.

4. Transfer the potato mixture to the air fryer basket. Air fry
for 18 to 20 minutes, pausing to shake the basket halfway
through the cooking time, until the potatoes are browned
and tender.

5. Transfer the fries to a large bowl and toss with the
cheese, rosemary, and truffle seasoning. Drizzle with truffle
oil (if using) just before serving.

CLASSIC POUTINE

MAKES
2 SERVINGS

PREP
15 MINUTES

TOTAL
35 MINUTES

2 russet potatoes

1 tablespoon olive oil

1 teaspoon salt

½ teaspoon freshly ground black pepper

1 (1.2-ounce) envelope brown gravy mix

½ cup cheese curds

Nothing says comfort food like this French-Canadian favorite featuring fries, gravy, and cheese curds. With a taste like mild cheddar and texture reminiscent of mozzarella, cheese curds are simply solid pieces of curdled milk that can be eaten plain or fried. (Fun fact: because fresh curds are porous with air trapped inside, they sometimes squeak when you bite into them.) Paired with a good lager, poutine is a cozy meal unto itself.

1. Preheat the air fryer to 400°F.

2. Cut the potatoes into French fry–size pieces (keep the skin on for extra flavor).

3. In a large bowl, toss the potatoes, olive oil, salt, and pepper until the potatoes are thoroughly coated.

4. Transfer the potato mixture to the air fryer basket. Air fry for 20 minutes, pausing to shake the basket halfway through the cooking time, until the potatoes are browned and tender.

5. Meanwhile, prepare the brown gravy according to package instructions.

6. Serve the fries topped with the gravy and cheese curds.

→ · SOUTHWESTERN · ←
EGG ROLLS

MAKES
4 SERVINGS

PREP
20 MINUTES

TOTAL
30 MINUTES

12 ounces leftover grilled sirloin, thinly sliced

1 cup shredded cheddar cheese

¼ cup thick salsa

3 scallions, thinly sliced

1 tablespoon chili powder

1 pound egg roll wrappers

1 egg, lightly beaten

Hot sauce (optional)

Thinly chopped chives (optional)

If you can roll, you can certainly put together a takeout favorite: egg rolls! The next time steak night comes around, grill some extra so you'll have leftovers handy for these delicious cheesy appetizers. If you're not a beef fan or you're looking to lower the cost, cooked chicken works well, too. Your air fryer makes it quick and simple to get right to the enjoyment.

· ◆ ·

1. Preheat the air fryer to 375°F.

2. In a large bowl, combine the steak, cheese, salsa, scallions, and chili powder. Stir until thoroughly combined.

3. Working one at a time, lay an egg roll wrapper diagonally in front of you (like a diamond). Add 2 heaping tablespoons of the beef filling in the middle. Fold the corner closest to you over the filling, and then fold in the sides.

4. Using a pastry brush, brush the remaining edges with the beaten egg, and then roll tightly like a burrito. Press the edges lightly to seal. When all of the egg rolls have been assembled, spritz generously with olive oil.

5. Working in batches if necessary, arrange the egg rolls in a single layer in the air fryer basket, leaving space in between the rolls. Air fry for 8 to 10 minutes, pausing halfway through the cooking time to flip the egg rolls, until golden brown.

6. Serve topped with a dash of hot sauce and chives (if using).

VEGETABLE SAMOSAS

►MAKES◄
12 SAMOSAS

►PREP◄
35 MINUTES

►TOTAL◄
45 MINUTES

½ pound yellow potatoes, coarsely chopped

3 tablespoons olive oil, divided

1 teaspoon curry powder

½ teaspoon salt

½ teaspoon grated fresh ginger

½ teaspoon cumin

⅓ cup frozen peas, thawed

¼ cup minced red onion

1 package pie dough

1 cup plain Greek yogurt (optional)

½ cup chutney (optional)

Packaged pie dough isn't just for sweet treats. These savory pastries explode with flavor and are the perfect addition to any menu when you want to impress. Your air fryer does all the heavy lifting where the cooking time is concerned, but you can also use it to reheat them if you want to make some ahead of time.

• • • • • • • • • • • • • • • • • • • ◆ •

1. Place the potatoes in a medium pot and fill with water until the potatoes are covered. Bring the water to a boil over high heat and cook 10 to 15 minutes, until the potatoes are soft. Drain the potatoes and return to the pot.

2. Using the back of a fork, coarsely mash the potatoes. Add 2 tablespoons of the olive oil along with the curry powder, salt, ginger, and cumin; mash again until thoroughly combined. Fold in the peas and onion. Set aside.

3. On a lightly floured work surface, working one piece at a time, roll out the pie dough into a thin oblong, approximately 18 inches long and 7 inches wide. Cut the dough into 6 roughly equal pieces, each approximately 6 inches long and 3½ inches wide. Repeat with the remaining dough to make 12 pieces. Fill a small bowl with water and set aside.

4. To shape and fill the samosas, working one at a time, form a cone by folding the short sides toward the center so that they overlap and create a point in the middle along one edge of one long side. Place about 1½ tablespoons of the potato filling in the center of the cone and fold the top sides over to enclose them. Dip your finger into the water and brush the edges lightly to seal the dough. Repeat with the remaining dough and filling to make 12 samosas. When all of the samosas have been assembled, brush lightly with the remaining oil.

5. Working in batches if necessary, arrange the samosas in a single layer in the air fryer basket, leaving space in between the samosas. Air fry at 375°F for 8 to 10 minutes, pausing halfway through the cooking time to flip the samosas, until golden brown and heated through.

6. Serve with yogurt and chutney on the side (if using).

GRUYÈRE ARANCINI

MAKES

4 SERVINGS

PREP

20 MINUTES

TOTAL

30 MINUTES

1 cup all-purpose flour

½ teaspoon salt

2 large eggs

¾ cup panko breadcrumbs

¼ cup finely grated Parmesan cheese

2 cups prepared risotto, chilled

8 ounces Gruyère cheese, cut into ½-inch cubes

You'll need a batch of leftover risotto to make these addictive air-fried balls of rice but go ahead and use your favorite packaged mix if you like. The key detail is that the cooked, starchy rice needs to be cold in order to transform it into arancini. Stuffed with cheese and coated in crispy breadcrumbs, these are well worth the effort.

· ··◆·· ·

1. Preheat the air fryer to 400°F.

2. In a shallow bowl, mix the flour and salt. Place the eggs in another shallow bowl and whisk until smooth. In a third shallow bowl, combine the breadcrumbs and Parmesan cheese; stir until thoroughly combined.

3. Scoop approximately 2 tablespoons of risotto into the palm of your hand. Place a cube of Gruyère in the middle, then roll into a ball, making sure to close the cheese completely into the ball. Set aside on a plate. Repeat with the remaining risotto.

4. Working one piece at a time, dredge the rice balls in the flour mixture, followed by the eggs, and finally roll them in the breadcrumb mixture, patting gently to ensure an even coating. Spritz generously with olive oil.

5. Working in batches if necessary, arrange the rice balls in a single layer in the air fryer basket, leaving space in between them. Air fry for 10 minutes, or until golden.

AIR-FRIED RAVIOLI
→ WITH MARINARA ←

MAKES
4 SERVINGS

PREP
20 MINUTES

TOTAL
30 MINUTES

1 cup seasoned breadcrumbs

¼ cup shredded
Parmesan cheese

2 teaspoons dried basil

½ cup all-purpose flour

2 large eggs, lightly beaten

1 package (9 ounces) frozen
beef ravioli, thawed

Fresh minced basil (optional)

1 cup marinara
sauce, warmed

This easy appetizer is perfect for a game-day get-together—premade ravioli makes it a cinch. Just a quick trip through the air fryer renders the cheese-filled pasta crispy and delicious. Once you get the hang of it, experiment with other flavor combinations—cheese ravioli dipped in basil sauce or a vegetable ravioli (like spinach or butternut) paired with Alfredo sauce.

1. Preheat the air fryer to 350°F.

2. In a shallow bowl, mix the breadcrumbs, cheese, and dried basil. In two additional bowls, place the flour and eggs separately. Working one piece at a time, dip the ravioli in flour to coat both sides; shake off the excess. Dip in the eggs, then dip in the breadcrumb mixture, patting gently to ensure an even coat. Spritz generously with olive oil.

3. Working in batches if necessary, arrange the ravioli in a single layer in the air fryer basket. Air fry for 8 to 10 minutes, pausing halfway through the cooking time to flip the ravioli, until golden.

4. Sprinkle with fresh basil (if using) and additional cheese. Serve with marinara for dipping.

→ GOLDEN ←
MAC & CHEESE BITES

MAKES
4 SERVINGS

PREP
20 MINUTES

TOTAL
30 MINUTES +
REFRIGERATION TIME

1½ cups elbow macaroni

1 cup chicken broth

½ cup heavy cream

¾ cup shredded
cheddar cheese

½ cup freshly shredded
mozzarella cheese

¼ cup freshly grated
Parmesan cheese

Kosher salt and freshly
ground black pepper

2 large eggs, beaten

1 cup panko breadcrumbs

Featuring bite-size morsels of America's favorite comfort food, these appetizer gems are delectable enrobed in a crispy exterior. Another great surprise: you don't need to worry about using a stovetop to boil the pasta beforehand.

. . . . ◆ . . . .

1. Preheat the air fryer to 350°F.

2. In a nonstick baking dish that fits your air fryer (at least 4 cups), combine the macaroni, broth, cream, cheeses, and salt and pepper to taste. Mix the ingredients until the macaroni is completely coated.

3. Place the pan in the air fryer basket. Air fry for 30 minutes, until the mac and cheese is bubbling and golden brown. Set aside to cool.

4. When cooled enough that the cheese is firm, use a 2-tablespoon cookie scoop to divide the mac and cheese into individual, bite-size pieces. Arrange them on a plate or cookie sheet, cover loosely with plastic wrap, and refrigerate until the balls are very firm, approximately 4 hours.

5. Whisk the eggs in a shallow bowl; place the breadcrumbs on a plate. Working one piece at a time, roll the mac and cheese bites between your hands to ensure a round shape. Dip each piece into the beaten egg, then roll it in the breadcrumbs to coat evenly. Spritz generously with olive oil.

6. Working in batches if necessary, arrange the balls in a single layer in the air fryer basket. Air fry at 400°F for 10 minutes, or until golden.

DELICIOUSNESS ON A STICK

→ POTATO CHIP ←
SKEWERS

MAKES

4 SERVINGS

PREP

20 MINUTES

TOTAL

40 MINUTES

2 Yukon Gold potatoes, skin pierced with a fork

¼ cup butter, melted

1 tablespoon garlic powder

1 tablespoon paprika

1 teaspoon salt

½ teaspoon freshly ground black pepper

¼ cup grated Parmesan cheese

Chopped fresh rosemary, for garnish

Ketchup

Homemade potato chips become an elevated eating experience when you spiral-cut and season them on a skewer. A short time in the microwave gives your potatoes a head start in cooking and makes them easier to skewer. Then the air fryer works its crisping magic with less fat and mess than traditional methods. If using wooden or bamboo skewers, always make sure to soak them in water beforehand to ensure they won't burn in the air fryer.

1. Soak two wooden skewers in water for 30 minutes. Preheat the air fryer to 350°F.

2. Microwave the potatoes for 1 to 1½ minutes, then leave them in the microwave for a few minutes to cool down and soften. When they are cool enough to handle, insert a wooden skewer into the bottom of each potato and gently push it all the way through the top. Hold a sharp, thin knife at an angle, and working in a spiral motion from one side to the other, cut in the opposite direction you are turning the skewered potato, cutting all the way down to the skewer. Take your time and work to make a thin, even spiral.

3. Gently fan out each potato down the length of the skewer, creating even gaps between the slices. Brush the melted butter all over the potatoes and sprinkle with garlic powder, paprika, salt, and pepper.

4. Arrange the potatoes in a single layer in the air fryer basket. Air fry for 20 minutes until browned.

5. Top with the cheese and rosemary. Serve with the ketchup on the side.

→ TERIYAKI ←
CHICKEN SKEWERS

MAKES
4 SERVINGS

PREP
10 MINUTES

TOTAL
25 MINUTES +
REFRIGERATION TIME

½ cup reduced-sodium soy sauce

¼ cup chicken broth

¼ cup orange juice

2 tablespoons brown sugar

1 tablespoon freshly grated ginger

1 tablespoon minced garlic

1 pound boneless, skinless chicken thighs, cut into 1-inch pieces

The simple secret to flavor success with this dish is allowing enough time for the marinade to work its magic. Because you're threading your skewers before placing the chicken in the marinade, there's no need to soak them beforehand if you're using wooden ones. If you're pressed for time, take a shortcut and use about a cup of store-bought marinade.

. . . . ◆ . . . .

1. In a resealable bag, combine the soy sauce, broth, orange juice, brown sugar, ginger, and garlic.

2. Thread the chicken pieces onto 8 skewers and add to the bag. Seal the bag and massage it lightly to ensure the chicken is evenly coated. Refrigerate for at least 1 hour, preferably overnight.

3. Working in batches if necessary, arrange the chicken in a single layer in the air fryer basket. Discard the marinade. Air fry at 350°F for 13 to 16 minutes, pausing halfway through the cooking time to flip the chicken, until the chicken is cooked through.

➤ ·ZESTY· ⬅
CHICKEN KEBABS

MAKES
4 SERVINGS

PREP
15 MINUTES

TOTAL
35 MINUTES +
REFRIGERATION TIME

2 pounds boneless, skinless chicken thighs, cut into 2-inch pieces

Juice of 1 lemon

2 tablespoons olive oil

1 tablespoon dried oregano

1 tablespoon garlic powder

1½ teaspoons salt

1 teaspoon paprika

1 teaspoon freshly ground black pepper

4 garlic naan

2 tablespoons butter, melted

Buttery, garlic naan, a type of Indian flatbread, is the perfect foil for these spicy chicken kebabs that come together super fast in the air fryer. You can add some vegetable toppings if you like—shredded lettuce, sliced tomato, a little diced red onion—but frankly these are irresistible just as they are presented here for their stunning simplicity and amazing flavor.

. . . . ◆ . . . .

1. Thread the chicken pieces onto 8 skewers. Place in a resealable bag.

2. In a small bowl, mix together the lemon juice, olive oil, oregano, garlic powder, salt, paprika, and pepper. Pour the marinade mixture over the chicken. Seal the bag and massage it lightly to ensure the chicken is evenly coated. Refrigerate for at least 1 hour, preferably overnight.

3. Working in batches if necessary, arrange the skewers in a single layer in the air fryer basket. Discard the marinade. Air fry at 400°F for 15 to 20 minutes, pausing to flip the skewers halfway through the cooking time, until the chicken is cooked through.

4. Warm the naan according to package instructions and brush with butter. Serve the chicken skewers alongside the naan.

→·HAWAIIAN·←
CHICKEN KEBABS

MAKES
4 SERVINGS

PREP
25 MINUTES

TOTAL
40 MINUTES +
REFRIGERATION TIME

¼ cup reduced-
sodium soy sauce

¼ cup pineapple juice

2 teaspoons sesame oil

1 tablespoon honey

1 teaspoon freshly
grated ginger

1 teaspoon minced garlic

1½ pounds boneless,
skinless chicken breasts,
cut into 1-inch chunks

1 medium red onion, cut
into 1-inch chunks (optional)

1½ cups pineapple chunks

2 red bell peppers, cut
into 1-inch chunks

1 teaspoon cornstarch

Hawaiian attire optional. Bring together sweet and salty
for a flavor party on a stick! These kebabs will deliver a
delicious taste of summer any time of year. If you can, use
fresh pineapple instead of the canned stuff—the results
are amazing. Serve with coconut rice for an absolute feast.

· ••◆•• ·

1. In a bowl, whisk together the soy sauce, pineapple juice,
sesame oil, honey, ginger, and garlic.

2. Place the chicken in a resealable bag along with half of
the soy sauce mixture. Cover and refrigerate the remaining
marinade for later. Refrigerate the chicken for at least 1 hour,
preferably overnight.

3. Soak 8 skewers in water for 30 minutes. Remove the
chicken from the marinade, and discard the marinade.

4. To assemble, alternate threading the chicken, onion
(if using), pineapple, and red pepper onto the skewers.
Working in batches if necessary, arrange the skewers in a
single layer in the air fryer basket. Air fry at 400°F for 12 to
15 minutes, pausing to flip the skewers halfway through the
cooking time, until the chicken is cooked through.

5. Meanwhile, make the sauce. Heat the remaining marinade
in a saucepan over medium-high heat. Whisk the cornstarch
with 1 tablespoon of water and add it to the pot. Bring to a
boil and stir frequently until it thickens and coats the back of
a spoon, about 1 minute. Remove from the heat.

6. Just before serving, brush the kebabs with the
thickened sauce.

→ THAI ←
CHICKEN STRIPS

MAKES
4 SERVINGS

PREP
25 MINUTES

TOTAL
40 MINUTES +
REFRIGERATION TIME

2 boneless, skinless chicken breasts (about 1½ pounds)

½ cup coconut milk

Juice and zest of 1 lime

2 tablespoons brown sugar

1 tablespoon curry powder

1 tablespoon minced garlic

1 tablespoon freshly grated ginger

1 tablespoon fish sauce

PEANUT SAUCE

½ cup crunchy peanut butter

1 tablespoon sesame oil

1 tablespoon oyster sauce

1 tablespoon sriracha

1 tablespoon brown sugar

2 teaspoons fish sauce

This combination of flavors is popular the world over for its intense mix of both sweet and spicy. Though these strips are often served straight from a grill, your air fryer can deliver the right amount of intense heat to produce great results. Threading the chicken strips onto a skewer makes them easier to turn, no matter what cooking device you use.

. . . . ◆ . . . .

1. Cut the chicken lengthwise into strips about ½-inch thick and thread onto 8 to 12 wooden skewers.

2. Place the chicken in a resealable bag. Add the coconut milk, lime juice and zest, brown sugar, curry powder, garlic, ginger, and fish sauce. Seal the bag and massage lightly to ensure the chicken is completely coated. Refrigerate for 1 hour.

3. Working in batches if necessary, arrange the skewers in a single layer in the air fryer basket. Discard the marinade. Air fry at 400°F for 12 to 15 minutes, pausing to flip the skewers halfway through the cooking time, until the chicken is cooked through.

4. Meanwhile, to make the peanut sauce: In a bowl, mix together the peanut butter, sesame oil, oyster sauce, sriracha, brown sugar, and fish sauce until smooth. Mix in warm water, a tablespoon at a time, to thin the sauce to desired consistency.

5. Serve the skewers with the peanut sauce.

STROMBOLI
→ ON A STICK ←

MAKES
4 SERVINGS

PREP
15 MINUTES

TOTAL
25 MINUTES +
SOAKING TIME

¼ cup unsalted butter, melted

¾ teaspoon garlic salt

1 tablespoon chopped
fresh basil

½ cup grated
Parmesan cheese

1 (13.8-ounce) package
pizza crust

16 slices (about ¼ pound)
deli ham or large pepperoni

1 cup marinara, warmed

If you enjoy the slightly crisp texture of pepperoni on a well-done pizza as much as you love the soft chewy quality of a breadstick, you know that getting both textures in one dish is rarely possible. However, sometimes a recipe comes along that proves you can have it all.

1. Soak 8 wooden skewers in water for 30 minutes. Preheat the air fryer to 400°F.

2. In a small bowl, mix together the butter, garlic salt, and basil. On a plate, scatter the cheese; set aside.

3. On a lightly floured surface, roll the pizza dough into a rectangle about 8 inches wide and 12 inches long. Brush the dough with the butter mixture; cut the dough into 8 strips about 1-inch wide.

4. Working one piece at a time, fold the ham or pepperoni and thread onto the skewers, leaving some space between the pieces so you can fan out the meat accordion style. Wrap a strip of dough around each skewer in a spiral motion; make sure the buttered side faces out. Pinch in the ends to secure the dough. Roll the skewers in the cheese to coat.

5. Working in batches if necessary, arrange the skewers in a single layer in the air fryer basket. Air fry for 10 to 12 minutes, pausing to flip the skewers halfway through the cooking time, until the dough is browned to your liking.

6. Serve with the marinara on the side.

COCONUT CHICKEN
→ WITH SPICY MANGO DIPPING SAUCE ←

MAKES
4 SERVINGS

PREP
15 MINUTES

TOTAL
30 MINUTES +
SOAKING TIME

1 egg

1 cup sweetened
coconut flakes

½ cup panko breadcrumbs

1 pound chicken tenders

½ teaspoon salt

¼ teaspoon freshly
ground black pepper

½ cup all-purpose flour

**SPICY MANGO
DIPPING SAUCE**

½ cup mayonnaise

½ mango, peeled and cubed

1 tablespoon fresh lime juice

1 tablespoon honey

1 tablespoon sriracha
(optional)

½ teaspoon curry powder

½ teaspoon salt

The contrast of tender, juicy chicken surrounded by a layer of crispy coating makes this dish an air fryer masterpiece. You don't necessarily need to serve the chicken on a stick, but it makes the presentation more fun and festive. Use as much or as little of the sriracha as desired, depending on how spicy you like your dishes.

1. Soak 4 wooden skewers in water for 30 minutes. Preheat the air fryer to 360°F.

2. Place the egg in a shallow bowl and beat it lightly. In another shallow bowl, mix the coconut and breadcrumbs.

3. Cut the chicken into large chunks and place in a large bowl. Sprinkle with salt and pepper until evenly coated. Add the flour and toss until the chicken is thoroughly coated. Thread the chicken pieces onto the wooden skewers.

4. Dip the skewers in the egg, then roll them in the coconut mixture, pressing firmly to ensure an even coating.

5. Arrange the chicken in a single layer in the air fryer basket. Air fry for 15 minutes, pausing halfway through the cooking time to flip the chicken, until the coating is golden and the chicken is cooked through.

6. To make the dipping sauce: In the work bowl of a food processor, combine the mayonnaise, mango, lime juice, honey, sriracha (if using), curry powder, and salt. Whirl until smooth.

7. Serve the chicken skewers with the dipping sauce.

→ ITALIAN ←
PORK & PEPPERS

MAKES
2 SERVINGS

PREP
10 MINUTES

TOTAL
25 MINUTES

1 pound garlic and rosemary marinated pork tenderloin, cut into 1- to 2-inch pieces

1 red bell pepper, cut into 1- to 2-inch pieces

1 yellow bell pepper, cut into 1- to 2-inch pieces

1 tablespoon olive oil

1 tablespoon Italian seasoning

Keeping it to five simple ingredients and three steps doesn't equate to any sacrifice in taste. It doesn't get easier than this—marinated pork tenderloin, conveniently packaged at the grocery store, is loaded with flavor. Just slice it up, thread it on to some skewers along with a couple of vegetables, and pop it in your air fryer for a quick and delicious weeknight meal.

1. Soak 4 wooden skewers in water for 30 minutes. Preheat the air fryer to 400°F.

2. Thread the pork and peppers onto the skewers. Brush with olive oil and sprinkle with the Italian seasoning.

3. Working in batches if necessary, arrange the skewers in a single layer in the air fryer basket. Air fry for 10 to 15 minutes, pausing to flip the skewers halfway through the cooking time, until the pork is cooked through and the vegetables are tender.

→ GROWN-UP ←
SAUSAGE ROLLS

› MAKES ‹
18 SERVINGS

› PREP ‹
15 MINUTES

› TOTAL ‹
40 MINUTES +
SOAKING TIME

18 fully cooked sausage links

1 large egg

1 tablespoon water

2 sheets frozen puff pastry
(from a 16- to 17.3-ounce
package), thawed
according to package
instructions, divided

¼ cup mustard

Ketchup (optional)

Remember loving "pigs in a blanket" when you were a kid? Those dressed-up hot dogs wrapped in a crescent roll? Well, here's to delighting your grown-up taste buds with some throwback fun. Puff pastry and any number of gourmet sausage combinations (think pineapple and bacon, or artichoke and garlic) elevate your memories into fine festive cuisine, and serving them on a stick makes them far easier to handle during a party.

· ·◆· ·

1. Soak 18 wooden skewers in water for 30 minutes. Thread each sausage lengthwise with a skewer.

2. In a small bowl, whisk the egg and water.

3. On a lightly floured surface, unfold 1 sheet of the puff pastry and gently roll it into a 12-inch square. Using a pizza wheel or sharp knife, cut the puff pastry into 9 (4-inch) squares. Brush half of each square with the mustard and the other half with the egg wash.

4. Place a sausage in the middle of each square. Fold the mustard side up over the sausage, then continue to roll toward the egg-wash side until the sausage is completely enclosed. Place on a baking sheet seam-side down. Repeat with the remaining ingredients.

5. Working in batches if necessary, arrange the skewers in a single layer in the air fryer basket. Air fry at 400°F for 20 to 25 minutes, pausing to flip the skewers halfway through the cooking time, until the dough is browned to your liking.

6. Serve with additional mustard and ketchup (if using).

→ SPICY BACON-WRAPPED ←
HOT DOGS

 MAKES
4 SERVINGS

PREP
10 MINUTES

TOTAL
25 MINUTES +
SOAKING TIME

8 slices bacon

8 hot dogs

4 dill pickle spears,
finely chopped

2 tablespoons pickled
jalapeño peppers,
finely chopped

2 tablespoons minced onion

8 hot dog rolls

Here's a fun way to put a delicious twist on your hot dogs—literally! Air fryers are legendary for providing a fuss-free way to cook bacon, so why not use yours for this super-easy treat? Threading your ingredients on a skewer may seem like a fussy step, but it's a great way to keep everything secure as the bacon will naturally shrink during cooking.

• •◆• •

1. Soak 8 wooden skewers in water for 30 minutes. Preheat the air fryer to 400°F.

2. Working one piece at a time, thread the end of a piece of bacon onto a skewer. Run the skewer lengthwise through the center of the hot dog just until the skewer is near the end of the hot dog. Wrap the bacon tightly around the hot dog so the bacon edges touch, but do not overlap, and then finish pushing the skewer the rest of the way through the hot dog, so that the bacon is secured at each end of the skewer. Repeat with the remaining bacon and hot dogs.

3. Working in batches if necessary, arrange the skewers in a single layer in the air fryer basket. Air fry at 400°F for 10 to 15 minutes, pausing to flip the skewers halfway through the cooking time, until the bacon is crisped to your liking.

4. Meanwhile, in a small bowl, mix together the pickles, jalapeños, and onion.

5. Place the hot dogs in the buns, remove the skewers, and serve with the pickle mixture.

→ FILIPINO BBQ ←
PORK SKEWERS

MAKES
4 SERVINGS

PREP
10 MINUTES

TOTAL
30 MINUTES +
MARINATING TIME

1½ pounds pork butt, cut into 1-inch cubes

¼ cup banana or tomato ketchup

½ cup lemon-lime soda

½ cup soy sauce

¼ cup rice vinegar

⅓ cup brown sugar

1 teaspoon freshly ground black pepper

2 large heads garlic, minced

SPICED VINEGAR DIP

½ cup white vinegar

2 cloves garlic, peeled and minced

¼ cup finely chopped sweet onion

1 Thai chili pepper, finely chopped

Salt and freshly ground black pepper

If you can find banana ketchup, available online and in well-stocked Asian groceries, the classic Filipino condiment adds a fruity twist to the marinade. However, in a pinch, tomato ketchup will work, too. The hands-on prep time is minimal, but this dish is best started the night before as the pork tastes best after marinating overnight.

· ◆ ·

1. Thread the pork cubes onto 8 skewers. Place in a resealable bag.

2. In a bowl, mix together the ketchup, soda, soy sauce, rice vinegar, brown sugar, pepper, and garlic. Pour the marinade mixture over the pork. Seal the bag and massage it lightly to ensure the pork is evenly coated. Refrigerate for at least 4 hours, preferably overnight.

3. Working in batches if necessary, arrange the skewers in a single layer in the air fryer basket. Discard the marinade. Air fry at 400°F for 15 to 20 minutes, pausing to flip the skewers halfway through the cooking time, until the pork is cooked through.

4. To make the dip: In a small bowl, combine the vinegar, garlic, onion, and pepper. Season to taste with salt and pepper.

5. Serve the pork skewers with the dip.

KOFTE KEBABS

MAKES
4 SERVINGS

PREP
15 MINUTES

TOTAL
25 MINUTES

1 teaspoon salt

1 teaspoon ground coriander

1 teaspoon ground cumin

½ teaspoon ground allspice

½ teaspoon ground turmeric

1 pound 85% lean ground beef

¼ cup chopped fresh parsley

2 cloves garlic, minced

1 tablespoon olive oil

Whether you choose to serve these dazzling kebabs on a bed of rice, tucked into a pita, or straight off a skewer, they never disappoint. And making them with an air fryer means your after-the-feast cleanup is kept to a minimum. For best results, use metal skewers with this recipe; if you must use wooden skewers, make sure to soak them in water for 30 minutes beforehand.

1. Preheat the air fryer to 370°F.

2. In a small bowl, combine the salt, coriander, cumin, allspice, and turmeric. Stir until thoroughly combined.

3. In a large bowl, combine the beef, spice mixture, parsley, and garlic. Mix with your hands until thoroughly combined.

4. Divide the mixture into 4 equal pieces and roll into thick logs. Using small metal skewers that will fit inside your air fryer, place each skewer lengthwise into the side of each log and use your hands to shape and press the meat around the skewer so that it looks as if you've threaded a sausage. Brush the kebabs with the olive oil.

5. Arrange the kebabs in a single layer in the air fryer basket. Air fry for 10 minutes, until the kebabs are cooked through and an instant-read thermometer inserted into the thickest portion registers 145°F.

→ SPANISH-STYLE ←
SHRIMP & SAUSAGE SKEWERS

MAKES
4 SERVINGS

PREP
10 MINUTES

TOTAL
20 MINUTES +
REFRIGERATION TIME

1 pound large shrimp (about 16–20), peeled and deveined

2 cloves garlic, finely minced

Juice of 1 lime

2 tablespoons olive oil

1 teaspoon smoked paprika

½ teaspoon salt

¼ teaspoon red pepper flakes

1 pound cured chorizo, sliced into 16 rounds

Zesty shrimp embracing seasoned sausage . . . so good! If you're planning a party, use large cocktail toothpicks instead of skewers and serve this dish in appetizer-size portions. Just make sure to soak the toothpicks in water as you would wooden skewers. And consider making a double batch—these are hard for a hungry crowd to resist.

. . . . ◆ . . . .

1. In a large bowl, combine the shrimp, garlic, lime juice, olive oil, paprika, salt, and pepper flakes. Mix until the shrimp are thoroughly coated. Cover and refrigerate for 30 minutes. Soak 8 wooden skewers in water for 30 minutes.

2. Preheat the air fryer to 400°F.

3. To assemble, thread alternating pieces of shrimp and chorizo onto the skewers so that the shrimp sits snugly between the sausage and curls around it. Discard the marinade.

4. Working in batches if necessary, arrange the skewers in a single layer in the air fryer basket. Air fry for 10 to 12 minutes, until the shrimp are pink and cooked through and the edges of the sausage are slightly crispy.

TACOS, SLIDERS, AND SANDWICHES

ROASTED CAULIFLOWER TACOS 54

FRESH FISH TACOS 57

ROASTED SWEET POTATO TACOS WITH LIME CREMA 58

KOREAN BEEF TACOS 59

BETTER-THAN-BACON PORK BELLY TACOS 61

DELUXE GRILLED HAM & CHEESE 62

AIR-FRIED EGGPLANT PARM SANDWICHES 63

BEST BARBECUE SLIDERS 65

NASHVILLE HOT CHICKEN SANDWICHES 66

HAWAIIAN CHICKEN BURGERS 69

MIDWESTERN PORK SANDWICHES 70

ANYTIME BREAKFAST SANDWICH 71

PORK BAHN MI 73

SHRIMP PO-BOYS 74

STREET CORNER CHEESESTEAKS 76

TRADITIONAL CUBANOS 77

BEEF GYROS WITH TZATZIKI SAUCE 78

→ ROASTED ←
CAULIFLOWER TACOS

MAKES
2 SERVINGS

PREP
15 MINUTES

TOTAL
35 MINUTES

1 small head cauliflower, cut into florets

2 tablespoons olive oil

2 tablespoons taco seasoning

¼ cup tahini

2 tablespoons fresh lime juice

1 teaspoon ground chipotle pepper

6 (6-inch) flour tortillas

2 radishes, thinly sliced

½ cup shredded red cabbage

Fresh cilantro, for garnish (optional)

Meatless Monday, Taco Tuesday . . . these super-easy vegan tacos make any dinner a delicious celebration. Seasoned roasted cauliflower atop warm tortillas is just the ticket for healthy flavor. And thanks to your air fryer, dinner for two can be ready in less time than ordering and picking up takeout.

1. Preheat the air fryer to 400°F.

2. In a large bowl, combine the cauliflower, olive oil, and taco seasoning, tossing gently until the cauliflower is evenly coated.

3. Transfer the cauliflower to the air fryer basket, spreading it into an even layer so that it cooks evenly. Air fry for 18 to 20 minutes, pausing to shake the basket halfway through the cooking time, until the cauliflower is fork tender and browned.

4. Meanwhile, in a small bowl, combine the tahini, lime juice, and chipotle pepper. Stir until smooth. Heat the tortillas according to package instructions.

5. To serve, divide the cauliflower among the tortillas, top with the radishes and cabbage, and drizzle with the tahini sauce. Garnish with cilantro (if using).

➤· FRESH ·◄
FISH TACOS

◄ MAKES ►
2 SERVINGS

◄ PREP ►
10 MINUTES

◄ TOTAL ►
25 MINUTES

1 pound cod fillets

1 tablespoon olive oil

2 tablespoons taco seasoning

¼ cup mayonnaise

2 tablespoons fresh lime juice

1 teaspoon minced garlic

6 (6-inch) flour tortillas

¼ cup thinly sliced red onion

¼ cup chopped fresh cilantro

Flesh of 1 avocado,
sliced (optional)

Craving the peace of the beach but can't get away? You can at least give your taste buds a trip to the beach when you bite into these luscious fish tacos. You'll also appreciate how cooking the fish so quickly in the air fryer means minimal mess and fewer fishy smells lingering in the kitchen.

1. Cut a piece of parchment paper to fit inside the air fryer basket. Preheat the air fryer to 350°F.

2. Place the cod on the parchment paper. Drizzle with the olive oil and sprinkle the taco seasoning on top. Spread the oil and seasoning gently to coat both sides of the fish.

3. Transfer the parchment paper to the air fryer basket. Air fry for 8 minutes, then pause the air fryer and flip the fish. Continue air frying for 5 to 7 minutes longer, or until the fish flakes easily with a fork.

4. Meanwhile, in a small bowl, combine the mayonnaise, lime juice, and garlic. Stir until smooth. Heat the tortillas according to package instructions.

5. To serve, divide the fish among the tortillas (cut into bite-size pieces if you prefer), and top with the mayonnaise sauce, onions, and cilantro. Serve with avocado slices (if using).

ROASTED SWEET POTATO TACOS
➤ WITH LIME CREMA ◄

MAKES
2 SERVINGS

PREP
15 MINUTES

TOTAL
35 MINUTES

1 large sweet potato, peeled and chopped

1 poblano chili pepper, seeded and chopped

1 tablespoon olive oil

2 teaspoons chili powder

Salt and freshly ground black pepper

1 tablespoon honey (optional)

6 (6-inch) flour tortillas

LIME CREMA

¼ cup plain Greek yogurt or sour cream

1 tablespoon mayonnaise

Zest of 1 lime

Step up and customize your order! You can create an infinite number of riffs on this dish. Need to stretch the servings? Toss in a can of black beans (rinsed and drained) when you pull the potatoes out of the air fryer. Find new pepper varieties at the farmers market? Toss them in! The natural sweetness of the potato will be amplified in the air fryer, so use honey only if you like the contrast of spicy and sweet to be well pronounced.

1. Preheat the air fryer to 370°F.

2. In a large bowl, combine the sweet potato, poblano chili pepper, olive oil, and chili powder, tossing gently until the vegetables are evenly coated. Season to taste with salt and pepper.

3. Transfer the vegetables to the air fryer basket, spreading them in an even layer. Air fry for 20 minutes, pausing to shake the basket halfway through the cooking time, until the potatoes are fork tender and browned. Transfer the cooked vegetables back to the bowl and drizzle with honey (if using), tossing gently until evenly coated.

4. Meanwhile, make the lime crema: In a small bowl, combine the yogurt, mayonnaise, and lime zest; season to taste with salt. Stir until smooth. Heat the tortillas according to package instructions.

5. To serve, divide the vegetables among the tortillas and top with the lime crema.

➤ KOREAN ⬻
BEEF TACOS

◆MAKES◆
2 SERVINGS

◆PREP◆
10 MINUTES

◆TOTAL◆
25 MINUTES +
MARINATING TIME

¾ pound sirloin, thinly sliced

½ sweet onion, thinly sliced

¼ cup bulgogi sauce

¼ cup mayonnaise

1 tablespoon sriracha

6 (6-inch) flour tortillas

½ cup kimchi

¼ cup chopped fresh cilantro

Seasoned sirloin tucked into a taco and topped with crunchy, spicy kimchi could be the ultimate flavor fusion. And it's so easy to enjoy at home with an air fryer—no waiting for an order to arrive. New to bulgogi sauce? It's a sweet Korean marinade that's widely available, and with good reason—it's delicious.

. . . . ◆ . . . .

1. In a large bowl, stir together the beef, onion, and bulgogi sauce until thoroughly combined. Cover and refrigerate for at least 30 minutes or up to 24 hours.

2. Preheat the air fryer to 400°F.

3. Transfer the meat mixture to the air fryer basket. Air fry for 12 minutes, pausing halfway through the cooking time to shake the basket, until the meat is browned and cooked through.

4. Meanwhile, in a small bowl, stir together the mayonnaise and sriracha until thoroughly combined. Warm the tortillas according to package instructions.

5. To serve, divide the meat among the tortillas and top with the sriracha-mayonnaise sauce, kimchi, and cilantro.

→ · BETTER-THAN-BACON · ←
PORK BELLY TACOS

MAKES
2 SERVINGS

PREP
20 MINUTES

TOTAL
45 MINUTES

1 pound pork belly

1 tablespoon olive oil

1 tablespoon ancho chile powder

2 teaspoons sugar

1 teaspoon salt

½ teaspoon ground cumin

6 (5-inch) flour tortillas, warmed

1 cup shredded cabbage (optional)

1 small tomato, chopped

⅓ cup finely chopped sweet onion

⅓ cup chopped fresh cilantro

2 fresh lime wedges

Pork belly is the cut that, when cured, becomes bacon—so you know these tacos will have incredible flavor. For this recipe, you'll use the fresh version of the meat and your own perfect seasoning blend to create a crispy yet juicy indulgence in the air fryer. Because pork belly is not cured, it doesn't have the additives and sodium most types of bacon have—making it a cleaner eating choice.

· ◆ ·

1. Preheat the air fryer to 325°F.

2. Cut the pork into ½-inch slices and then crosswise into 1-inch pieces. Place in a large bowl and drizzle with the olive oil, tossing to coat. Add the ancho chile powder, sugar, salt, and cumin. Toss again until the pork is thoroughly coated with the spices.

3. Transfer the pork to the air fryer basket and arrange in a single layer. Air fry for 20 to 25 minutes, pausing to shake the basket several times during the cooking time, until the pork begins to brown and become crisp.

4. Meanwhile, warm the tortillas according to package instructions.

5. To serve, divide the pork among the tortillas and top with the cabbage (if using), tomato, onion, cilantro, and lime.

→ · DELUXE · ←
GRILLED HAM & CHEESE

MAKES
1 SANDWICH

PREP
5 MINUTES

TOTAL
15 MINUTES

1 tablespoon mayonnaise

2 slices whole wheat bread

1 tablespoon fig jam

2 ounces thinly
sliced deli ham

2 slices thinly sliced Havarti

Your air fryer is your new best friend when it comes to making just about any version of a grilled cheese sandwich, but this particular pairing of salty ham and sweet fig jam is over the top. Using a light coating of mayonnaise on your bread in place of butter renders a perfect crisp, but butter is still always a classic option.

1. Preheat the air fryer to 370°F.

2. Spread the mayonnaise on one side of each piece of bread. Stack them together so the mayonnaise is on the inside.

3. Spread the jam on the top slice of the bread stack and layer the ham and cheese on top. Lift the top slice of bread with the topping and place in the air fryer basket. Cover with the remaining slice of bread (mayonnaise side on top). Air fry for 8 minutes, pausing halfway through the cooking time to flip the sandwich.

4. Carefully remove from the air fryer, slice in half, and enjoy immediately.

AIR-FRIED EGGPLANT
PARM SANDWICHES

MAKES
4 SANDWICHES

PREP
20 MINUTES

TOTAL
35 MINUTES

1 medium eggplant, sliced into ½-inch rounds

1 teaspoon salt

1 cup panko breadcrumbs

¼ cup grated Parmesan cheese

1 teaspoon Italian seasoning

¼ cup all-purpose flour

1 teaspoon garlic powder

2 eggs

4 sub rolls

1 cup marinara

1 cup shredded mozzarella cheese

Craving a classic Italian sandwich? Your air fryer has you covered—it's the perfect appliance to make this crispy classic in record time. Very little oil is needed, making the results healthier and the process less messy.

1. Preheat the air fryer to 370°F.

2. Place the eggplant slices in a colander and sprinkle with the salt. Set the colander aside over a large bowl.

3. In a wide, shallow bowl, combine the breadcrumbs, cheese, and Italian seasoning; stir until thoroughly combined and set aside. In another shallow bowl, combine the flour and garlic powder; stir until thoroughly combined and set aside. In a third shallow bowl, whisk the eggs.

4. Blot the eggplant dry with a paper towel. Working one slice at a time, dredge the eggplant first in the flour mixture, then in the beaten eggs, and finally in the breadcrumb mixture, patting gently to ensure an even coating.

5. Working in batches if necessary, spritz the eggplant slices with olive oil and arrange in a single layer in the air fryer basket so the slices do not touch. Air fry for 12 minutes, pausing halfway through the cooking time to flip the eggplant, until the coating is browned and the eggplant fork tender.

6. Meanwhile, split open the rolls and spread ¼ cup of the marinara inside each roll.

7. Use tongs to carefully place the eggplant in the rolls. Top with the cheese and air fry again for 3 to 4 minutes, until the cheese is melted and the bread is toasted.

→ BEST ←
BARBECUE SLIDERS

MAKES
2 SANDWICHES

PREP
10 MINUTES

TOTAL
20 MINUTES

2 cups shredded chicken

½ cup prepared
barbecue sauce

1 tablespoon olive oil

1 teaspoon cider vinegar

1 teaspoon honey

1 cup shredded coleslaw mix

Salt and freshly ground
black pepper

2 brioche rolls

We all know that barbecue sliders are an easy solution for leftover cooked rotisserie chicken. However, what you may not appreciate (until you try this sandwich) is that the results in an air fryer are far superior to what you can do with a microwave because the barbecue sauce has an opportunity to thicken into a juicy glaze with just a hint of crispiness.

. . . . ◆ . . . .

1. Preheat the air fryer to 400°F.

2. In a small baking dish, mix the chicken and barbecue sauce, stirring with a fork until the meat is thoroughly coated. Scatter the meat in a single layer in the air fryer basket (don't press it down; leave some clumps so there's more surface area for the air fryer to caramelize). Air fry for 8 minutes, until the chicken is warmed through and the sauce has begun to thicken.

3. Meanwhile, in a medium bowl, whisk together the olive oil, vinegar, and honey. Add the coleslaw mix and toss until thoroughly coated. Season to taste with salt and pepper.

4. Divide the chicken between the brioche rolls and top with the coleslaw mix.

→ NASHVILLE HOT ←
CHICKEN SANDWICHES

·MAKES·	·PREP·	·TOTAL·
4 SANDWICHES	15 MINUTES	30 MINUTES + MARINATING TIME

4 boneless, skinless chicken breast cutlets (about 1½ pounds)

2 tablespoons pickle juice, divided

2 tablespoons hot sauce, divided

1¼ cups all-purpose flour

Salt and freshly ground black pepper

½ cup buttermilk

1 egg

4 tablespoons butter

1 tablespoon brown sugar

2 teaspoons cayenne

1 teaspoon garlic powder

1 teaspoon paprika

4 brioche buns

Dill pickle slices

1 cup creamy coleslaw

Pickle juice is the secret (sensational!) ingredient in this sandwich that's coated with a double layer of seasoned flour and then dressed in a sweet-hot sauce. With an air fryer you can skip the mess of deep-frying altogether. Pick up some ready-made coleslaw in your grocer's deli case, and you're ready to roll.

· ◆ ·

1. In a resealable bag, combine the chicken, 1 tablespoon of the pickle juice, and 1 tablespoon of the hot sauce. Massage the bag to ensure the chicken is thoroughly coated. Refrigerate for at least 1 hour or overnight.

2. Preheat the air fryer to 380°F.

3. Place the flour in a shallow bowl and season to taste with salt and pepper. In another shallow bowl, whisk together the remaining pickle juice and hot sauce, the buttermilk, and the egg. Working one piece at a time, dredge the chicken first in the seasoned flour, followed by the buttermilk, and then in the flour once more. Arrange on a plate and repeat with the remaining cutlets. Spritz the chicken generously with olive oil.

4. Working in batches if necessary, arrange the chicken in a single layer in the air fryer basket, making sure the pieces do not to overlap. Air fry for 12 minutes, pausing to flip the chicken halfway through the cooking time, until the coating is browned and an instant-read thermometer inserted into the thickest piece registers 165°F.

5. While the chicken is cooking, prepare the butter sauce. In a small saucepan on medium heat, melt the butter and stir in the brown sugar, cayenne, garlic powder, and paprika. Remove from the heat and keep warm until the chicken is done.

6. Brush the cutlets generously with the butter sauce.

7. To assemble the sandwiches, line the bottom buns with pickles, add the cutlets, and top with the coleslaw.

➤· HAWAIIAN ·◄
CHICKEN BURGERS

MAKES
2 SANDWICHES

PREP
10 MINUTES

TOTAL
25 MINUTES

2 boneless, skinless chicken breast cutlets (about ¾ pound)

2 thick slices red onion

Salt and freshly ground black pepper

2 slices pineapple

2 sesame sandwich rolls

¼ cup barbecue sauce

½ cup baby greens

2 slices cheddar cheese

This sandwich gets a huge flavor boost from its many toppings, so there's no need to season the chicken beyond simple salt and pepper. Just load everything into your air fryer and you're practically done. Serve with a side of sweet potato chips.

1. Preheat the air fryer to 380°F.

2. Season the chicken and onion slices with salt and pepper to taste. Spritz generously with olive oil.

3. Arrange the chicken, onion, and pineapple in the air fryer basket. Air fry for 12 minutes, pausing to flip the chicken halfway through the cooking time, until the chicken is cooked through and an instant-read thermometer inserted into the thickest piece registers 165°F.

4. To assemble the sandwiches, split the rolls and spread a tablespoon of barbecue sauce on each side. Divide the greens among the rolls and top with chicken, the cheese, onion, and pineapple.

→ MIDWESTERN ←
PORK SANDWICHES

MAKES · 2 SANDWICHES

PREP · 15 MINUTES

TOTAL · 25 MINUTES

2 (6-ounce) boneless pork chops

½ teaspoon salt

¼ teaspoon freshly ground black pepper

¼ cup flour

1 egg

½ cup panko breadcrumbs

2 sandwich buns

Yellow mustard

6 dill pickle slices

These babies are built for a healthy appetite. You will get the classic taste without the greasy mess of deep-frying thanks to your air fryer. As they're traditionally served, the thin and crispy piece of pork is far bigger than the sandwich roll and should hang over the sides.

. . . . ◆ . . . .

1. Preheat the air fryer to 400°F.

2. Working one at a time, place each pork chop between 2 sheets of parchment paper and use the flat side of a meat mallet to pound them to ¼-inch thickness. Season both sides of the chops with the salt and pepper; sprinkle with the flour and spread with your hands to make sure the chops are thoroughly coated.

3. In a shallow bowl, whisk the egg. Place the breadcrumbs on a plate. Dredge the chops in the egg, followed by the breadcrumbs. Pat gently to ensure an even coating. Spritz generously with olive oil.

4. Working in batches if necessary, arrange the pork in a single layer in the air fryer basket. Air fry for 10 minutes, pausing halfway through the cooking time to flip the chops, until cooked through.

5. Serve on the buns topped with yellow mustard and the pickles.

➤ ANYTIME ❖
BREAKFAST SANDWICH

MAKES
1 SANDWICH

PREP
5 MINUTES

TOTAL
15 MINUTES

1 large egg

Salt and freshly ground black pepper

1 (1-ounce) frozen fully cooked breakfast sausage patty

1 English muffin, split

2 teaspoons butter, softened

1 slice American cheese

Air fryers are the perfect appliance for quick meals like this because you can load everything into the basket and there's no standing in front of a skillet—and thus no dirty skillet to wash. Make this one for breakfast or any time the craving hits.

· ❖ ·

1. Preheat the air fryer to 350°F.

2. Center a mason jar lid, upside down, on a 5-inch square of aluminum foil. Fold the foil up and around the lid to act as a round mold. Spritz the foil and lid with olive oil and crack the egg into the center. Season to taste with salt and pepper.

3. Split the English muffin and spread with the butter.

4. Place the egg mold and frozen sausage patty next to each other in the air fryer basket; air fry for 4 minutes. Flip the sausage patty over, add the English muffin halves, and air fry for 4 minutes more.

5. To assemble the sandwich, carefully run a knife along the outside edge of the ring mold to loosen the egg. Set one half of the English muffin on top; using a pot holder to protect your hands, carefully flip the ring mold to remove the egg. Top with the cheese, sausage patty, and remaining English muffin half.

PORK BAHN MI

◄MAKES►
2 SANDWICHES

◄PREP►
10 MINUTES

◄TOTAL►
30 MINUTES + MARINATING TIME

2 cloves garlic, minced

1½ teaspoons Chinese five spice powder

2 tablespoons brown sugar

1 tablespoon soy sauce

1 tablespoon hoisin sauce

1 tablespoon vegetable oil

1 tablespoon fresh lime juice

½ cup + 1 tablespoon rice vinegar, divided

1 pound pork tenderloin

1 carrot, shredded

½ cup thinly sliced cucumber

¼ cup thinly sliced onion

¼ cup mayonnaise

1 tablespoon sriracha

1 (12-inch) baguette, halved

¼ cup fresh cilantro

2 tablespoons sliced jalapeño pepper (fresh or pickled)

There are endless combinations of flavorful ingredients that can be loaded into this classic Vietnamese sandwich, but this version represents all the delicious basics you'll need to enjoy a perfect version straight from your air fryer.

. . . . ••◆•• . . . .

1. In a baking dish that will fit your air fryer, whisk together the garlic, five spice powder, brown sugar, soy sauce, hoisin sauce, oil, lime juice, and 1 tablespoon vinegar. Add the pork to that dish and turn to coat completely with the marinade. Let sit at room temperature for up to 30 minutes, turning occasionally.

2. Preheat the air fryer to 400°F.

3. Place the baking dish in the air fryer and air fry for about 20 minutes, pausing halfway through the cooking time to flip the meat, until an instant-read thermometer inserted into the thickest portion registers 145°F. Remove from the air fryer and let rest for 5 to 10 minutes before slicing thinly. Reserve the thickened marinade to spoon onto the sandwiches if you like.

4. While the pork is cooking, combine the carrot, cucumber, onion, and the remaining ½ cup vinegar in a bowl and toss to coat. In a small bowl, combine the mayonnaise and sriracha. Set aside.

5. To assemble the sandwiches, drain the vegetables. Split each baguette half and press open like a book. Spread the mayonnaise mixture over the bread and top with layers of pork, vegetables, cilantro, and jalapeño slices.

SHRIMP PO-BOYS

MAKES
2 SANDWICHES

PREP
10 MINUTES

TOTAL
20 MINUTES

½ cup all-purpose flour

2 teaspoons Cajun seasoning, divided

1 egg

1 cup panko breadcrumbs

¾ pound large shrimp, peeled and deveined

⅓ cup mayonnaise

1 tablespoon dill pickle relish

1 teaspoon fresh lemon juice

1 teaspoon capers, drained and coarsely chopped

Dash of hot sauce

2 (8-inch) baguettes, split horizontally

¼ cup chopped fresh parsley

1 small tomato, thinly sliced (optional)

½ cup shredded iceberg lettuce (optional)

According to local legend, these sandwiches got their name in New Orleans when a restaurant started giving them for free to hungry streetcar workers during a strike. But there's a good reason these humble sandwiches have stood the test of time and become popular all over the nation—they're incredibly hearty and delicious. And with an air fryer at your disposal, you can enjoy one whenever you like!

1. Preheat the air fryer to 325°F.

2. In a wide, shallow bowl, combine the flour and 1½ teaspoons of the Cajun seasoning; stir until thoroughly combined and set aside. In another shallow bowl, whisk the egg. In a third shallow bowl, place the breadcrumbs.

3. Blot the shrimp dry with a paper towel. Working a few pieces at a time, dredge the shrimp first in the flour mixture, then in the beaten egg, and finally in the breadcrumbs, patting gently to ensure an even coating. Spritz the shrimp generously with olive oil.

4. Working in batches if necessary, arrange the shrimp in a single layer in the air fryer basket so they do not touch. Air fry for 8 to 10 minutes, pausing halfway through the cooking time to flip the shrimp, until the shrimp are cooked through and the breading is crispy..

5. Meanwhile, in a small bowl, combine the mayonnaise, relish, lemon juice, capers, remaining ½ teaspoon Cajun seasoning, and hot sauce; stir until thoroughly combined. Split open the baguettes and spread the mayonnaise mixture evenly in each baguette. Top with the shrimp, parsley, tomato slices (if using), and lettuce (if using).

→ STREET CORNER ←
CHEESESTEAKS

MAKES
2 SANDWICHES

PREP
15 MINUTES

TOTAL
30 MINUTES +
MARINATING TIME

1 beef rib-eye steak, thinly sliced (about ½ pound)

1 tablespoon Worcestershire sauce

2 teaspoons reduced-sodium soy sauce

½ sweet onion, thinly sliced

½ bell pepper, thinly sliced

2 teaspoons olive oil

¼ teaspoon salt

2 hoagie rolls

2 slices provolone cheese

The thinly sliced, tender steak, sautéed peppers and onions, and melted cheese that define Philadelphia-style cheesesteaks usually come together on a stovetop. However, there's no reason not to rely on your air fryer for equally delicious results. To get super-thin pieces of meat, place your steak in the freezer for 15 to 20 minutes before slicing.

. . . . ◆ . . . .

1. In a resealable bag, combine the steak, Worcestershire sauce, and soy sauce. Seal the bag and refrigerate for at least 4 hours, preferably overnight.

2. Preheat the air fryer to 400°F.

3. In a large bowl, combine the onion, pepper, olive oil, and salt. Toss until the vegetables are thoroughly coated. Transfer the vegetables to the air fryer basket and air fry for 5 minutes, until the vegetables begin to soften. Scatter the meat on top of the vegetables and air fry for another 5 minutes, until the meat is browned and cooked through. Discard the marinade.

4. Divide the meat and vegetables between the hoagie rolls. Top with the cheese slices.

5. Working in batches if necessary, return the sandwiches to the air fryer basket and air fry at 400°F for 2 to 3 minutes, until the cheese is melted and the bread lightly toasted.

→ TRADITIONAL ←
CUBANOS

MAKES
2 SANDWICHES

PREP
10 MINUTES

TOTAL
45 MINUTES +
MARINATING TIME

2 tablespoons orange juice

1 tablespoon olive oil

1 teaspoon ground cumin

1 teaspoon smoked paprika

½ teaspoon salt

¼ teaspoon red pepper flakes

4 cloves garlic,
minced, divided

1 pound pork tenderloin

3 tablespoons mayonnaise

2 ciabatta rolls, split

¼ pound sliced deli ham

2 slices Swiss cheese

6 dill pickle slices

1 tablespoon yellow mustard

Few sandwiches are as satisfying as a well-made Cubano—layers of tender roast pork and ham under a blanket of melted Swiss with some pickles and mustard for good measure. While debate remains about the origins, the combination of flavors rarely disappoints. ¡Buen provecho!

1. In a resealable bag, combine the orange juice, olive oil, cumin, paprika, salt, pepper flakes, and half of the garlic. Add the pork tenderloin and massage to coat. Refrigerate for at least 4 hours, preferably overnight.

2. Preheat the air fryer to 400°F.

3. Transfer the pork to the air fryer basket and discard the marinade. Air fry the pork for 20 minutes, pausing halfway through the cooking time to flip the meat, until an instant-read thermometer inserted into the thickest portion of the tenderloin registers 145°F. Let rest for 5 to 10 minutes before slicing thinly.

4. While the pork is cooking, combine the remaining garlic and the mayonnaise in a shallow bowl. Set aside.

5. To assemble the sandwiches, spread the mayonnaise mixture across the bottom of each ciabatta roll and top with the sliced pork, ham, cheese, and pickles. Spread the mustard on the top half of the roll and press the sandwich to secure the ingredients.

6. Working in batches if necessary, return the sandwiches to the air fryer basket and air fry at 400°F for 5 to 6 minutes, until the cheese is melted and the bread lightly toasted.

BEEF GYROS
→ WITH TZATZIKI SAUCE ←

MAKES
2 SANDWICHES

PREP
15 MINUTES

TOTAL
20 MINUTES +
MARINATING TIME

1 beef rib-eye steak, thinly sliced (about ½ pound)

1 tablespoon olive oil

Juice of ½ lemon

3 cloves garlic, minced

1 teaspoon dried oregano

¼ teaspoon salt

2 pitas

½ cup shredded lettuce

¼ cup thinly sliced sweet onion

TZATZIKI SAUCE

½ cucumber, seeded and shredded

¼ teaspoon salt

½ cup plain Greek yogurt

2 tablespoons finely chopped fresh mint or dill

2 teaspoons fresh lemon juice

1 clove garlic, minced

In the restaurant world, gyro meat is roasted slowly over a spit, offering up small bits of well-done beef or lamb within each tender strip that's piled into a sandwich. That same contrast is easy to achieve in your own kitchen with this much-easier-to-prepare air fryer version. You can save valuable time without sacrificing taste!

1. In a resealable bag, combine the steak, olive oil, lemon juice, garlic, oregano, and salt. Seal the bag, massaging gently to ensure the meat is evenly coated, and refrigerate for at least 4 hours, preferably overnight.

2. To make the tzatziki sauce, place the cucumber in a colander and sprinkle with the salt. Let sit for 10 minutes, then squeeze gently to remove as much liquid as possible. Place in a small bowl and stir in the yogurt, mint or dill, lemon juice, and garlic. Cover and refrigerate until you're ready to serve.

3. Preheat the air fryer to 400°F.

4. Scatter the meat in the air fryer basket. Discard the marinade. Air fry for 5 to 7 minutes, pausing halfway through the cooking time to shake the basket, until the meat is browned and cooked through.

5. Warm the pitas according to package instructions.

6. Divide the meat between the pitas and top with the lettuce, onion, and tzatziki sauce.

WINGS AND THINGS

KOREAN CHICKEN WINGS 82

AIR-FRIED TANDOORI CHICKEN 85

DRY RUB CHICKEN WINGS 86

PECAN-CRUSTED CHICKEN TENDERS
WITH MAPLE-MUSTARD
DIPPING SAUCE 87

SPICY JERK CHICKEN 88

PERUVIAN CHICKEN
WITH AJI SAUCE 89

CLASSIC CHICKEN & WAFFLES 90

AIR-FRIED TIROPITA 93

BEEF EMPANADAS 94

JAMAICAN BEEF PIES 96

CHEESE TAQUITOS 98

REUBEN STROMBOLI 99

MEXICAN STREET CORN 101

ANY-TIME-OF-DAY
CHILAQUILES 102

VEGETABLE CALZONES 105

BIG EASY CRAB CAKES 106

FISH & CHIPS WITH
TARTAR SAUCE 108

➤ KOREAN ◄
CHICKEN WINGS

MAKES
2 SERVINGS

PREP
15 MINUTES

TOTAL
40 MINUTES

2 pounds chicken wings, tips removed

½ teaspoon salt

¼ teaspoon freshly ground black pepper

3 tablespoons cornstarch

2 tablespoons gochujang Korean chili paste

1 tablespoon honey

1 tablespoon mayonnaise

1 tablespoon ketchup

1 tablespoon sesame oil

2 teaspoons freshly grated ginger

2 teaspoons rice wine vinegar

1 tablespoon furikake or toasted sesame seeds (optional)

2 large scallions, thinly sliced (optional)

Chicken wings are beloved around the world, so there are a lot of varieties to choose from. However, this version takes its cues from the distinct flavor of a fermented chili paste known as gochujang. Available in most Asian food markets, gochujang is also easy to find online.

1. Preheat the air fryer to 350°F.

2. In a large bowl, toss the chicken wings with the salt, pepper, and cornstarch until thoroughly coated.

3. Working in batches if necessary, arrange the chicken in a single layer in the air fryer basket. Air fry for 25 minutes, pausing halfway through the cooking time to flip the chicken, until the wings are crisp and golden and an instant-read thermometer inserted into the thickest piece registers 165°F.

4. Meanwhile, in another large bowl, whisk together the gochujang, honey, mayonnaise, ketchup, oil, ginger, and vinegar.

5. Transfer the wings to the gochujang sauce and toss until the wings are thoroughly coated. Serve topped with the furikake or sesame seeds (if using) and the scallions (if using).

→ AIR-FRIED ←
TANDOORI CHICKEN

 MAKES
2 SERVINGS

 PREP
10 MINUTES

 TOTAL
30 MINUTES +
MARINATING TIME

¼ cup Greek yogurt

1 tablespoon minced ginger

1 tablespoon minced garlic

1 tablespoon lemon juice

1 tablespoon garam masala

1 tablespoon smoked paprika

1 tablespoon
ground coriander

1½ teaspoons salt

6 skinless chicken legs or
thighs (about 1½ pounds)

¼ cup thinly sliced red
onions, for garnish (optional)

4 lemon wedges, for garnish

This dish gets its name from a tandoor, a special kind of clay oven used in Indian cooking that exposes foods to remarkably high heat. Although scaled-down versions of tandoors are available, an air fryer does the job quite nicely too.

1. In a small bowl, whisk together the yogurt, ginger, garlic, lemon juice, garam masala, smoked paprika, coriander, and salt until thoroughly combined.

2. Place the chicken in a large resealable bag and add the yogurt mixture. Massage the bag to ensure the chicken is thoroughly coated. Seal the bag and refrigerate for at least 2 hours, preferably overnight.

3. Preheat the air fryer to 380°F.

4. Working in batches if necessary, arrange the chicken in a single layer in the air fryer basket. Discard the marinade. Air fry for 20 minutes, pausing halfway through the cooking time to flip the chicken, until the chicken is cooked through and an instant-read thermometer inserted into the thickest piece registers 165°F.

5. Serve with sliced red onions (if using) and lemon wedges.

→ DRY RUB ←
CHICKEN WINGS

MAKES
2 SERVINGS

PREP
10 MINUTES

TOTAL
35 MINUTES +
MARINATING TIME

1 tablespoon paprika

1 tablespoon sugar

½ teaspoon dried oregano

½ teaspoon garlic powder

½ teaspoon freshly
ground black pepper

½ teaspoon cayenne

1 pound chicken wings,
tips removed

⅓ cup prepared barbecue
sauce (optional)

4 ribs celery, cut into
4-inch pieces

½ cup blue cheese
or ranch dressing

How big is our national chicken wing obsession? According to some estimates, close to 1.5 billion wings are typically consumed during the weekend of that big football game. But you don't need to wait around for a game day party or make a trek to your local wing joint to enjoy this favorite appetizer. Your air fryer is always ready and waiting.

1. In a large bowl, mix together the paprika, sugar, oregano, garlic powder, pepper, and cayenne. Add the chicken wings and toss until thoroughly coated. Cover and refrigerate for at least 1 hour or up to 8 hours.

2. Preheat the air fryer to 400°F.

3. Working in batches if necessary, arrange the chicken in a single layer in the air fryer basket. Air fry for 25 minutes, pausing halfway through the cooking time to flip the chicken, until the wings are crisp and golden and an instant-read thermometer inserted into the thickest piece registers 165°F.

4. Transfer the wings to another large bowl and toss with the barbecue sauce (if using).

5. Serve with the celery and blue cheese or ranch dressing on the side.

PECAN-CRUSTED CHICKEN TENDERS
➜· WITH MAPLE-MUSTARD DIPPING SAUCE ·←

·MAKES·
4 SERVINGS

·PREP·
10 MINUTES

·TOTAL·
25 MINUTES +
MARINATING TIME

1 cup pecans

½ cup flour

2 eggs

1½ pounds chicken tenders

1 teaspoon salt

½ teaspoon freshly
ground black pepper

**MAPLE-MUSTARD
DIPPING SAUCE**

½ cup maple syrup

2 tablespoons Dijon mustard

Sure, it's easy to throw a batch of frozen chicken fingers into an air fryer and call it a meal. But why resort to that when a homemade version like this offers so much more flavor and takes only 10 minutes to put together? It's even faster than takeout!

1. Preheat the air fryer to 400°F.

2. In the work bowl of a food processor fitted with a metal blade, pulse the pecans until finely chopped. Tip the pecans onto a large plate and set aside. In a shallow bowl, place the flour. In another shallow bowl, beat the eggs with a fork until smooth.

3. Season the chicken with the salt and pepper. Working one piece at a time, dredge the chicken in the flour, followed by the eggs, and finally in the pecans, patting gently to ensure an even coating. Spritz the chicken generously with olive oil.

4. Working in batches if necessary, arrange the chicken in a single layer in the air fryer basket, making sure not to crowd the basket. Air fry for 10 to 12 minutes, pausing halfway through the cooking time to flip the chicken, until cooked through and an instant-read thermometer inserted into the thickest piece registers 165°F.

5. While the chicken is cooking, make the dipping sauce: In a small bowl, combine the syrup and mustard. Whisk until smooth.

6. Serve the tenders with the dipping sauce on the side.

→ SPICY ←
JERK CHICKEN

· MAKES ·
4 SERVINGS

· PREP ·
10 MINUTES

· TOTAL ·
35 MINUTES +
MARINATING TIME

3 tablespoons brown sugar

2 teaspoons salt

1 teaspoon ground allspice

1 teaspoon ground cinnamon

1 teaspoon ground ginger

1 teaspoon dried thyme

1 teaspoon cayenne

2 pounds bone-in
chicken pieces

This versatile recipe works with whatever part of the chicken you like—and it's your call if you want to keep the skin on or go skinless. Just make sure the pieces are of a uniform size, so your air fryer cooks them evenly. If using split chicken breasts, cut them in half crosswise and they'll cook a little faster. But whatever you do, don't go with boneless chicken. The bone helps impart a good deal of flavor.

• •◆• • • • • • • • • • • • • • • • • • • •

1. In a small bowl, combine the brown sugar, salt, allspice, cinnamon, ginger, thyme, and cayenne. Mix until thoroughly combined.

2. Use paper towels to pat the chicken dry. Cover the chicken with the spice mixture and massage until thoroughly coated. Place the chicken in a resealable bag and seal it shut. Refrigerate for 4 hours, preferably overnight.

3. Preheat the air fryer to 380°F.

4. Working in batches if necessary, arrange the chicken in a single layer in the air fryer basket, making sure not to crowd the basket. If using skinless chicken, spritz generously with olive oil. Air fry for 20 to 25 minutes, pausing halfway through the cooking time to flip the chicken, until cooked through and an instant-read thermometer inserted into the thickest piece registers 165°F.

PERUVIAN CHICKEN
→ · WITH AJI SAUCE · ←

MAKES
2 SERVINGS

PREP
10 MINUTES

TOTAL
35 MINUTES +
MARINATING TIME

Juice of 1 lemon

1 tablespoon olive oil

3 cloves garlic, minced

1 tablespoon ground cumin

1 tablespoon paprika

½ teaspoon freshly
ground black pepper

½ teaspoon dried oregano

1 teaspoon salt

4 skin-on chicken
thighs (about 1½ pounds)

AJI SAUCE

1 cup fresh cilantro

1 or 2 jalapeños, seeds
removed and coarsely
chopped

1 clove garlic

1 tablespoon olive oil

1 tablespoon fresh lime juice

¼ teaspoon kosher salt

⅓ cup mayonnaise

This dish, popular in Peruvian restaurants, is actually credited to a Swiss restaurateur who lived in Peru. He also had a hand in inventing the modern rotisserie ovens that are designed to roast chicken to golden perfection. However, an air fryer, with its ability to circulate warm air all around a dish as it cooks, works to similar effect.

1. In a small bowl, whisk together the lemon juice, olive oil, garlic, cumin, paprika, pepper, oregano, and salt.

2. Slip a finger underneath the chicken skin to loosen it and allow the marinade to better permeate. Place the chicken in a resealable bag and add the lemon mixture. Seal the bag and massage until the chicken is thoroughly coated. Refrigerate for at least 4 hours, preferably overnight.

3. Preheat the air fryer to 380°F.

4. Working in batches if necessary, arrange the chicken in a single layer in the air fryer basket, making sure not to crowd the basket. Discard the marinade. Air fry for 25 minutes, pausing halfway through the cooking time to flip the chicken, until cooked through and an instant-read thermometer inserted into the thickest piece registers 165°F.

5. Meanwhile, make the aji sauce: In the work bowl of a food processor fitted with a metal blade, combine the cilantro, jalapeños, garlic, olive oil, lime juice, salt, and mayonnaise. Whirl until smooth.

6. Serve the chicken with the aji sauce on the side.

→ CLASSIC ←
CHICKEN & WAFFLES

 MAKES
2 SERVINGS

 PREP
15 MINUTES

 TOTAL
45 MINUTES +
MARINATING TIME

1 pound bone-in, skin-on chicken thighs

½ cup buttermilk

1 tablespoon hot sauce

1 teaspoon salt, divided

1 cup all-purpose flour

1 tablespoon Old Bay seasoning

1 egg

4 preprepared or frozen waffles

¼ cup maple syrup

1 tablespoon butter

½ teaspoon cayenne (optional)

This brunch favorite will add fun and flavor to any meal! Make ahead a well-loved waffle recipe or use a frozen variety. The crisy chicken will be the real star!

· ◆ ·

1. In a large bowl or resealable bag, combine the chicken thighs, buttermilk, hot sauce, and ½ teaspoon of the salt. Mix until the chicken is thoroughly coated. Cover and refrigerate for at least 1 hour, preferably overnight.

2. Preheat the air fryer to 380°F.

3. In a shallow bowl, combine the remaining ½ teaspoon of salt, flour, and Old Bay seasoning and mix until thoroughly combined. In another shallow bowl, whisk the egg.

4. Remove the chicken from the buttermilk marinade, and discard the marinade. Dredge the chicken in the flour mixture until thoroughly coated. Dredge the chicken in the egg, followed by the flour mixture once more. Place the chicken on a plate and spritz generously with olive oil.

5. Arrange the chicken in the air fryer basket and air fry for 25 to 30 minutes, pausing halfway through the cooking time to flip the chicken, until browned and an instant-read thermometer inserted into the thickest piece registers 165°F.

6. Meanwhile, toast the waffles. In a small pan, warm the syrup, butter, and cayenne (if using) over medium heat until the syrup is warm and the butter has melted.

7. Serve the chicken sandwiched between the waffles, and top with the syrup mixture.

AIR-FRIED TIROPITA

MAKES
30 TIROPITA

PREP
30 MINUTES

TOTAL
45 MINUTES

3 eggs

½ pound feta cheese, crumbled

½ pound small-curd cottage cheese

¾ teaspoon salt, divided

8 ounces frozen phyllo dough, thawed

6 tablespoons salted butter, melted

½ cup Greek yogurt

1 tablespoon fresh lemon juice

1 tablespoon fresh thyme or dill, chopped

If you're a fan of savory Greek pastries, let your air fryer make it easy to prepare these cheese-and-egg-filled phyllo triangles! Bonus: you can make them ahead and keep them in your freezer—a perfect appetizer is always at the ready.

1. Preheat the air fryer to 350°F.

2. In a bowl, whisk the eggs until smooth. Add the cheeses and ½ teaspoon of salt and stir until thoroughly combined.

3. On a large cutting board, lay one sheet of phyllo horizontally in front of you. Brush generously with butter and lay another sheet on top. Use a knife or kitchen shears to cut the dough into 6 equal strips.

4. Place a small spoonful of the cheese mixture at the end of each strip. To assemble the tiropita, consider the proper way to fold a flag and work one at a time. Simply fold the bottom right corner over so that it meets the opposite edge of the strip and forms a 45-degree angle on the bottom left side of the strip. Fold again, this time flipping the triangle at its top edge. Continue folding and repeat with the remaining ingredients; arrange on a baking sheet and brush the tops of the tiropita with the remaining butter. (If you wish to freeze some of the tiropita at this point, place the baking sheet in the freezer for about an hour and then transfer to a freezer bag for long-term storage.)

5. Working in batches, arrange the tiropita in a single layer in the air fryer basket. Air fry for 12 to 15 minutes (or about 20 minutes if previously frozen), until golden. Transfer to a baking rack and cool briefly.

6. Meanwhile, in a small bowl, combine the yogurt, lemon juice, thyme or dill, and the remaining ¼ teaspoon of salt. Stir until thoroughly combined and serve alongside the tiropita.

BEEF EMPANADAS

MAKES
10 EMPANADAS

PREP
30 MINUTES

TOTAL
1 HOUR

1 pound 93% lean ground beef

1 small red bell pepper, finely chopped

1 small white onion, finely chopped

2 cloves garlic, minced

1 teaspoon ground cumin

1 teaspoon dried oregano

½ teaspoon salt

½ teaspoon paprika

1 (14-ounce) package frozen empanada dough, thawed

1 egg, lightly beaten

These meat-filled pastries are popular throughout Central and South America and contain a wide variety of subtleties in the seasoning mix depending on the region, so if you like this version you might want to explore other similar recipes. If you don't have a crowd to feed, these reheat well in the air fryer, too.

· ◆ · · · · · · · · · · · · · · · ·

1. Preheat the air fryer to 400°F.

2. In a large bowl, combine the beef, peppers, onions, garlic, cumin, oregano, salt, and paprika. Mix with wet hands until thoroughly combined.

3. Scatter the beef in small clumps in the air fryer and cook for 15 minutes until browned.

4. Transfer the beef to a bowl. Use a fork to mash the meat mixture until the beef is finely crumbled; let cool. When the air fryer is cool enough to handle, drain the drippings and wash the basket.

5. To assemble, place a disk of empanada dough in front of you. Brush the outer edge with the egg and place a spoonful of the meat mixture in the center. Fold in half to enclose the ingredients; use a fork to crimp the edges and to poke a few small holes in the top. Brush the tops with the egg, if desired, and spritz generously with olive oil. Repeat with the remaining ingredients.

6. Preheat the air fryer again to 400°F.

7. Working in batches if necessary, arrange the empanadas in a single layer in the air fryer basket. Air fry for 10 to 15 minutes, pausing halfway through the cooking time to flip the pastries, until lightly browned.

JAMAICAN BEEF PIES

MAKES
10 PIES

PREP
55 MINUTES

TOTAL
1 HOUR 30 MINUTES

2 cups all-purpose flour

2½ teaspoons Jamaican curry powder, divided

Pinch of salt

¼ cup butter

¼ cup lard

⅓ cup cold water

1 pound 93% lean ground beef

1 small onion, diced

1 teaspoon dried thyme

½ teaspoon salt

2 tablespoons beef broth

½ cup seasoned breadcrumbs

1 egg, lightly beaten

If you're a fan of Caribbean food, you're likely familiar with these amazing flavor bombs. The secret is that both the dough and beef filling are loaded with Jamaican curry powder. The Jamaican version has a slightly different mix of spices than a traditional Indian curry powder, so don't substitute here unless absolutely necessary. If, however, you're not a fan of using lard in your cooking, regular shortening will work just fine.

. . . . ◆ . . . .

1. In a large bowl, combine the flour, 1½ teaspoons curry powder, and salt. Use 2 knives to cut the butter and lard into the flour until the mixture resembles coarse crumbs. Stir in the water a few tablespoons at a time until the mixture forms a ball. Shape the dough into a log and cut it into 10 equal pieces. Cover loosely with a towel and set aside.

2. In another large bowl, combine the beef, onions, thyme, and salt. Mix with wet hands until thoroughly combined. Scatter the beef in small clumps in the air fryer and cook at 400°F for 15 minutes until browned.

3. Transfer the beef to a clean bowl and add the broth and breadcrumbs. Use a fork to gently mash the beef until the mixture is finely crumbled. When the air fryer is cool enough to handle, drain the drippings and wash the basket.

4. To assemble the pies, on a lightly floured surface, roll each dough piece into a 6-inch circle (approximately ⅛-inch thick).

5. Spoon equal amounts of filling onto each pastry circle. Fold over and press the edges together, making a half-circle. Use the back of a fork to seal the edges, then brush the tops with the egg.

6. Working in batches if necessary, arrange the pies in a single layer in the air fryer basket. Air fry at 400°F for 20 to 25 minutes, pausing halfway through the cooking time to flip the pies, until browned.

⟫ CHEESE ⟪
TAQUITOS

MAKES
2 SERVINGS

PREP
10 MINUTES

TOTAL
20 MINUTES

6 (6-inch) corn tortillas

1 tablespoon olive oil

6 (1-ounce) mozzarella cheese sticks

3 tablespoons canned green chiles, chopped, divided

Chili powder

½ cup green or red salsa

¼ cup finely chopped sweet onion

⅓ cup sour cream

Taquitos, which literally means "little tacos," are kind of like a cousin to the beloved restaurant standby. They have the same basic ingredients as tacos, but taquitos involve rolling the filling inside the tortilla before everything is fried together into crispy perfection. To make another satisfying version, just add some chopped cooked chicken.

· · · · · · · · · · · · · · · · · · · ·•◆•·· ·

1. Preheat the air fryer to 400°F.

2. Heat the tortillas according to package instructions.

3. Working one tortilla at a time, brush both sides with olive oil. Place a cheese stick near the center of the tortilla and 1½ teaspoons of the green chiles alongside the cheese. Roll the tortilla up tightly and place seam-side down in the air fryer basket. Repeat with the remaining ingredients.

4. Sprinkle the tortillas with a dash of chili powder and air fry for 7 to 10 minutes, until the tortilla begins to brown.

5. Let the taquitos sit in the air fryer basket for a few minutes before serving on a plate topped with the salsa, onions, and sour cream.

→ REUBEN ←
STROMBOLI

MAKES
4 STROMBOLI

PREP
10 MINUTES

TOTAL
25 MINUTES

1 pound pizza dough, thawed

1 cup shredded Swiss cheese

1 cup sauerkraut, drained

12 ounces thinly sliced pastrami

1 egg, lightly beaten

1 tablespoon caraway seeds

½ cup Thousand Island dressing

Part of the fun of eating out lies in the unique flavor combinations you can find. This take on stromboli calls for some surprise ingredients to blend a popular sandwich with the dough creation. It's loaded with pastrami, sauerkraut, and Swiss in place of the usual Italian fixings.

. . . . ◆ . . . .

1. Preheat the air fryer to 370°F.

2. Divide the pizza dough into 4 pieces. On a lightly floured surface, roll each into a rectangular shape, about 8 inches long and 6 inches wide.

3. Scatter the cheese along the length of each piece of dough, followed by the sauerkraut. Arrange the pastrami on top, concentrating the meat on one side and leaving about 1 inch of the dough free of all toppings.

4. Carefully roll the stromboli jelly roll–style. Tuck the ends inward and continue rolling until all the ingredients are enclosed. Pinch the seams closed.

5. Brush the top of each stromboli with the egg and sprinkle with the caraway seeds. Use a sharp knife to make a few shallow slashes in the top of each stromboli.

6. Working in batches if necessary, arrange the stromboli in the air fryer basket with room in between. Air fry for about 10 to 15 minutes, pausing halfway through the cooking time to flip the stromboli, until golden.

7. Serve the stromboli with the dressing on the side.

→ MEXICAN ←
STREET CORN

MAKES
4 SERVINGS

PREP
5 MINUTES

TOTAL
20 MINUTES

4 ears corn on the cob, husks and silks removed

3 tablespoons butter, melted

⅓ cup sour cream

1 teaspoon chili powder

¼ teaspoon kosher salt

¼ teaspoon freshly ground black pepper

½ cup crumbled cotija or grated Parmesan cheese

¼ cup chopped fresh cilantro

½ lime, cut into wedges (optional)

This popular version of corn on the cob (also known as *elote*) is often grilled, but it's simple to put together with an air fryer—any time of year, in any weather. Every bite pops with flavor! Cotija is a Mexican cow's milk cheese that's delicious atop all sorts of foods, from soups to tacos to salads.

. . . . ◆ . . . .

1. Preheat the air fryer to 400°F.

2. Brush the corn with the melted butter (reserve any butter that remains). Working in batches if necessary, arrange the corn in a single layer in the air fryer basket and air fry for 10 to 15 minutes, pausing every 5 minutes to turn the corn.

3. Meanwhile, combine the sour cream, chili powder, salt, and pepper with the remaining butter; mix until thoroughly combined.

4. To serve, drizzle or brush the corn with the sour cream mixture and sprinkle with the cheese and cilantro. Serve with the lime wedges (if using) to squeeze over the top.

→ ANY-TIME-OF-DAY ←
CHILAQUILES

◄ MAKES ►
1 SERVING

◄ PREP ►
5 MINUTES

◄ TOTAL ►
15 MINUTES

2 ounces tortilla chips

½ cup green salsa

¼ cup thinly sliced red onion

1 large egg

2 tablespoons crumbled feta or cotija cheese

Breakfast foods can hit the spot any time of day! If you're tired of the traditional eggs and toast routine, here's a quick and easy way to spice things up with your air fryer. It takes just a few minutes to assemble this dish, but its comfort and satisfaction are sure to linger far longer.

1. Preheat the air fryer to 350°F.

2. Spritz a small baking dish that fits in your air fryer basket with olive oil.

3. In a large bowl, add the tortilla chips and salsa. Toss gently until the chips are thoroughly coated.

4. Transfer the chip mixture to the prepared baking dish. Scatter the onions on top. Make a well in the chip mixture and crack the egg in the indentation.

5. Place the dish in the air fryer basket and air fry for 5 to 10 minutes, until the egg is cooked to your preferred doneness and the tortillas are softened and crispy at the edges.

6. Top the dish with the cheese just before serving.

VEGETABLE CALZONES

MAKES
4 CALZONES

PREP
15 MINUTES

TOTAL
45 MINUTES

1 small white onion, chopped

8 ounces brown mushrooms, sliced

1 red bell pepper, seeded and thinly sliced

1 tablespoon olive oil

Salt and freshly ground black pepper

3 ounces baby spinach

½ cup ricotta

2 teaspoons minced garlic

1 pound pizza dough, thawed

1 cup shredded mozzarella cheese, divided

1 egg, lightly beaten

¼ cup grated Parmesan cheese

1 cup marinara sauce, warmed

One of the challenges in making a good vegetable calzone: the vegetables can get watery if they're not cooked well before you load them into the crust. With your air fryer, you'll get the perfect balance of fluffy on the inside and crispy on the outside.

1. Preheat the air fryer to 400°F.

2. In a large bowl, combine the onion, mushrooms, bell pepper, olive oil, and salt and pepper to taste. Toss until the vegetables are thoroughly coated.

3. Transfer the vegetable mixture to the air fryer basket. Air fry for 10 to 15 minutes, pausing every 5 minutes to shake the basket, until the vegetables are tender.

4. Transfer the cooked vegetables back to the bowl and add the spinach, ricotta, and garlic. Stir until thoroughly combined and the spinach is wilted.

5. Divide the pizza dough into 4 pieces. On a lightly floured surface, roll each into a round, about ¼-inch thick or less. Fill the center of each round with the vegetable mixture and top with ¼ cup of the mozzarella cheese. Fold the round in half, crimping the edges with a fork so they're closed and a half-moon shape is formed.

6. Brush the top of each calzone with the egg.

7. Set the air fryer to 370°F. Working in batches if necessary, place the calzones in the air fryer basket with room in between. Air fry for about 10 to 15 minutes, pausing halfway through the cooking time to flip the calzones, until golden.

8. Sprinkle with the Parmesan cheese and serve with the marinara on the side.

→ ·BIG EASY· ←
CRAB CAKES

·MAKES·
4 SERVINGS

·PREP·
20 MINUTES

·TOTAL·
35 MINUTES +
REFRIGERATION TIME

½ cup mayonnaise

2 tablespoons Dijon mustard

1 tablespoon Cajun seasoning

Zest of 1 lemon

2 (8-ounce) cans crabmeat, drained and picked over to remove any bits of shell

2 eggs

1 cup panko breadcrumbs, divided

½ teaspoon salt

Fresh parsley, for garnish (optional)

Sure, the name of this recipe is a reference to the great city of New Orleans, but the truth is, these delicious crab cakes are both big and easy to make in their own right. *Laissez les bon temps rouler!*

· · · · · · · · · · · · · · · · · · ◆ · · · · · · · · · · · · · · · · · · ·

1. Preheat the air fryer to 350°F.

2. In a large bowl, combine the mayonnaise, mustard, Cajun seasoning, and lemon zest. Stir until smooth. Transfer half of the mayonnaise mixture to a small serving bowl; cover and refrigerate until you're ready to serve.

3. Add the crabmeat, eggs, ½ cup of the breadcrumbs, and salt to the remaining mayonnaise mixture. Use a silicone spatula to gently fold until thoroughly combined, taking care not to break up the crabmeat too much. Cover and refrigerate for about an hour to allow the flavors to combine.

4. Cut a piece of parchment paper to fit the dimensions of your air fryer. Use an ice cream scoop to form 8 crab mixture patties and arrange on the paper so they do not touch. Use the bottom of the scoop to flatten the patties into a circle about ½-inch thick. Place the remaining breadcrumbs on top and spritz generously with olive oil. Air fry for 10 to 15 minutes, until lightly browned.

5. Serve the patties with the remaining mayonnaise sauce; garnish with fresh parsley (if using).

FISH & CHIPS
➤ WITH TARTAR SAUCE ◄

MAKES	PREP	TOTAL
4 SERVINGS	10 MINUTES	45 MINUTES

2 russet potatoes, peeled (about 1 pound)

1 tablespoon olive oil

1½ teaspoons salt, divided

1½ pounds cod fillets

½ teaspoon freshly ground black pepper

¼ cup flour

2 eggs

1 cup panko breadcrumbs

Lemon slices, for garnish

TARTAR SAUCE

½ cup sour cream

½ cup mayonnaise

2 tablespoons chopped dill pickle

1 tablespoon capers, drained and chopped

Here's an interesting bit of food lore: the beloved combination of fried fish served on a bed of French fries was once considered so important to national morale that it was one of the few foods the British government refused to ration during World War II. Fortunately, a few things have changed since then. You can enjoy this treat from your air fryer anytime—and without an oily mess. Keep cooking and carry on!

. . . . ◆ . . . .

1. Preheat the air fryer to 400°F.

2. Cut the potatoes into French fry–size pieces. Drizzle with the olive oil and sprinkle with ½ teaspoon of the salt. Toss to coat.

3. Scatter the fries in a single layer in the air fryer basket. Air fry for 20 minutes, pausing halfway through the cooking time to shake the basket. When the fries are cooked through and brown, transfer to a serving bowl and cover with foil to keep warm.

4. Meanwhile, season the cod with the remaining teaspoon of salt and the black pepper. Sprinkle with the flour until thoroughly coated; set aside.

5. In a shallow bowl, lightly beat the eggs. In a second shallow bowl, place the breadcrumbs.

6. Working with a few pieces at a time, dip the fish into the egg mixture followed by the breadcrumbs. Press lightly to ensure an even coating. Spritz generously with olive oil.

7. Arrange the fish in a single layer in the air fryer basket. Air fry for 12 to 15 minutes at 400°F, pausing halfway through the cooking time to flip the fish, until the fish flakes easily with a fork.

8. Meanwhile, make the tartar sauce: In a small bowl, combine the sour cream, mayonnaise, pickle, and capers. Stir until smooth.

9. Serve the fish piled atop the fries with the tartar sauce on the side. Garnish with the lemon slices.

SWEET TREATS

→ · CHERRY · ←
HAND PIES

· MAKES ·
8 HAND PIES

· PREP ·
15 MINUTES

· TOTAL ·
30 MINUTES

1 (14-ounce) package refrigerated pie crust

½ cup all-fruit cherry preserves or cherry pie filling

1 egg, lightly beaten

2 tablespoons sugar

Perfectly portioned for single servings and easy to put together with an air fryer, these pies travel well and are an ideal treat to take along on a picnic or to a tailgate party. For a shiny sparkle of sugar on top, as in this photo, use coarse decorating sugar; however, Demerara sugar, or even regular granulated sugar, will taste just as good.

· ◆ ·

1. Preheat the air fryer to 350°F.

2. Roll out the pie crusts on a lightly floured surface. Use a sharp knife to cut 4 circles from each crust; discard the edges.

3. Place a tablespoon of preserves or filling in the center of each crust. Working one at a time, fold opposite sides of the dough toward the center and pinch the seam closed to form a football-shaped pie. Crimp the edges with a fork. Use the tip of a knife to cut a small hole in the top so steam can escape. Brush the pies with the egg and sprinkle with the sugar.

4. Working in batches if necessary, arrange the pies in the air fryer basket so they do not touch. Air fry for 10 to 15 minutes, until golden.

5. Serve warm or at room temperature.

→ GUAVA ←
HAND PIES

› MAKES ‹
8 HAND PIES

› PREP ‹
15 MINUTES

› TOTAL ‹
30 MINUTES

1 (14-ounce) package refrigerated pie crust

¼ cup guava paste

½ cup whipped pineapple cream cheese

1 cup powdered sugar

2 tablespoons milk

1 teaspoon vanilla extract

Try something beyond the traditional fruit pies! Guava paste is usually easy to find wherever Latin ingredients are sold. Just a little cream cheese in the center balances out the intensely sweet and slightly flowery flavor of guava.

1. Preheat the air fryer to 350°F.

2. Roll out the pie crusts on a lightly floured surface. Trim each crust into a square and cut into 4 smaller squares for a total of 8 squares; discard the edges.

3. Place 1½ teaspoons of guava paste and a tablespoon of cream cheese in the center of each square. Working one at a time, fold one corner of the dough over and press against the opposite corner to form a triangle. Crimp the edges with a fork. Use the tip of a knife to cut a small hole in the top so steam can escape.

4. Working in batches if necessary, arrange the pies in the air fryer basket so they do not touch. Air fry for 10 to 15 minutes, until golden. Transfer to a baking rack and let cool.

5. Meanwhile, in a small bowl, combine the powdered sugar, milk, and vanilla. Stir until smooth, then drizzle over the cooled hand pies.

→ PEANUT BUTTER & ←
BANANA ROLLS

 MAKES
4 ROLLS

 PREP
10 MINUTES

 TOTAL
20 MINUTES

4 egg roll wrappers

2 tablespoons peanut butter

2 bananas, halved crosswise

1 tablespoon honey

Pinch of ground cinnamon

1 tablespoon canola oil

2 tablespoons
powdered sugar

¼ cup whipped cream

¼ cup hot fudge sauce,
warmed (optional)

If you have a few leftover egg roll wrappers and a couple of bananas handy, you have the main ingredients for this easy-to-put-together treat. It's a great sweet ending to a meal, or just a nice little snack whenever the craving hits. And with an air fryer at your disposal, these are ready in minutes.

· · · · · · · · · · · · · · · · · · · ◆ ·

1. Preheat the air fryer to 380°F.

2. Lay the egg roll wrappers diagonally in front of you (like a diamond). Spread 1½ teaspoons of the peanut butter in the middle of each wrapper and top with half of a banana. Drizzle with the honey and sprinkle with the cinnamon.

3. Put a small amount of water in a small bowl. Working with one egg roll wrapper at a time, fold the side closest to you in, and then bring in the sides. Roll tightly like a burrito. Dip your finger into the water and moisten the edges before pressing lightly to seal. Repeat with the remaining egg rolls. Brush the rolls with the oil.

4. Working in batches if necessary, arrange the rolls in a single layer in the air fryer basket with space in between the rolls. Air fry for 5 to 7 minutes, pausing halfway through the cooking time to flip the rolls, until golden brown.

5. Serve sprinkled with the powdered sugar and topped with the whipped cream and hot fudge sauce (if using).

→ ALL-AMERICAN ←
APPLE DUMPLINGS

MAKES	PREP	TOTAL
2 SERVINGS	15 MINUTES	40 MINUTES

2 small baking apples, such as Granny Smith

½ (14-ounce) package refrigerated pie crust

¼ cup brown sugar

¼ teaspoon ground cinnamon

Pinch of salt

2 tablespoons unsalted butter

1 tablespoon heavy cream

1 tablespoon granulated sugar

Vanilla ice cream (optional)

While apple pie will probably always remain a national favorite, there's a good reason to love apple dumplings. All the same flavors are baked into individual portions that are hearty and delicious. Fortunately, you can make them pretty easily in an air fryer, especially if you rely on prepared pie crust to give you a head start. Make sure to use a baking dish to collect any of the sauce that may leak out. You won't want to miss a drop.

· ◆ ·

1. Preheat the air fryer to 320°F.

2. Use a sharp knife to carefully remove the core and seeds from the center of the apples. Roll out the pie crust on a lightly floured surface. Divide the crust into 2 equal portions and set an apple in the center of each piece. Fill the center of each apple with the brown sugar, cinnamon, and salt. Top with butter.

3. Working one at a time, fold the dough up over the sides of the apple and pinch it closed at the top. If necessary, cover any gaps by pulling scraps of dough off the top and affixing them with a finger dipped in water. Use the tip of a knife to cut a small hole in the top so steam can escape.

4. Arrange the dumplings in a small baking dish that fits in the air fryer. Brush with the heavy cream and sprinkle with the granulated sugar. Air fry for 25 minutes, until the pastry is golden.

5. Serve topped with any accumulated juices as well as ice cream (if using).

→ · STRAWBERRY · ←
SHORTCAKE

MAKES
4 SERVINGS

PREP
20 MINUTES

TOTAL
40 MINUTES

3 cups sliced strawberries

3 tablespoons honey, divided

1 cup all-purpose flour, plus more for dusting

¼ cup sugar

2 teaspoons baking powder

¼ teaspoon salt

4 tablespoons butter, cut into 4 pieces

1 cup heavy cream, divided

½ teaspoon vanilla extract

Summer tastes like a big juicy serving of strawberry shortcake! Baking your own fresh-from-the-oven version doesn't mean you have to heat up the kitchen—just turn to your air fryer to make it simple with less heat.

· ◆ ·

1. In a large bowl, combine the strawberries and 1 tablespoon of the honey. Stir until the strawberries are thoroughly coated. Set aside.

2. Preheat the air fryer to 400°F.

3. In another large bowl, combine the flour, sugar, baking powder, and salt. Add the butter and work it into the flour mixture with your fingers until it resembles coarse meal. Make a well in the flour mixture and add ⅓ cup of the cream in the center. Stir just until dough forms.

4. Turn the dough onto a lightly floured work surface and divide into 4 pieces. Shape each piece into a biscuit about ½-inch thick.

5. Arrange the biscuits in the air fryer basket so they do not touch. Air fry for 15 to 20 minutes, until golden.

6. Meanwhile, in a large bowl, whip the remaining ⅔ cup of cream until soft peaks form. Add the remaining 2 tablespoons of the honey and the vanilla and continue whipping until stiff peaks form.

7. When the biscuits are cool enough to handle, split them in half. Divide the strawberries and any accumulated juices among the biscuits and top with the whipped cream before serving.

BOOZY BREAD PUDDING
➤ WITH BOURBON SAUCE ◄

MAKES
2 SERVINGS

PREP
15 MINUTES

TOTAL
30 MINUTES

2 tablespoons raisins

2 tablespoons bourbon

¼ cup heavy cream

¼ cup milk

2 tablespoons sugar

1 tablespoon butter, melted

1 large egg

1 cup day-old bread cubes (about 2 slices)

BOURBON SAUCE

2 tablespoons butter

⅓ cup packed brown sugar

1 tablespoon heavy cream

Reserved bourbon (from the soaked raisins)

Pinch of salt

Got a few slices of bread starting to go stale? This is your lucky day, because you probably also have almost everything else you need to put together this rich, comforting dessert. And it will only require about 15 minutes in the air fryer to reward you with its sinful sweetness.

. . . . ••◆•• . . . .

1. Preheat the air fryer to 325°F.

2. Coat 2 (8- to 10-ounce) ramekin baking dishes with butter and set aside.

3. In a small bowl, cover the raisins with the bourbon. Set aside.

4. In a large bowl, whisk together the cream, milk, sugar, butter, and egg until smooth. Add the bread cubes and stir until the bread is thoroughly coated. If the bread is particularly stale, let it sit for a few minutes until it begins to soak up the liquid. Drain the raisins (reserving the bourbon) and stir into the bread mixture until well combined.

5. Divide the bread mixture between the ramekin dishes.

6. Place the ramekins in the air fryer basket and air fry for 12 to 14 minutes, until the pudding is puffed and golden brown.

7. Meanwhile, make the bourbon sauce: In a small heavy saucepan over medium heat, combine the butter, brown sugar, cream, and reserved bourbon. Cook, stirring constantly, until the mixture comes to a boil and the sugar is completely dissolved. Remove from the heat and stir in the salt.

8. Pour the sauce over the puddings and serve warm.

→ NO-STRESS ←
DOUGHNUTS

· MAKES ·
4 DOUGHNUTS

· PREP ·
10 MINUTES

· TOTAL ·
20 MINUTES

1 cup all-purpose flour

1 tablespoon sugar

1½ teaspoons baking powder

½ teaspoon salt

¾ cup plain Greek yogurt

1 teaspoon vanilla extract

GLAZE

½ cup powdered sugar

1 tablespoon unsalted butter, melted

1½ teaspoons hot water

½ teaspoon vanilla extract

1–2 drops food coloring (optional)

Edible accents (optional)

Fresh doughnuts are a simply fantastic way to start the morning. If you make your own, the reward is double: not only do you get to enjoy delicious doughnuts, but you can stay in your pajamas instead of going out to fetch them from a bakery. Any type of plain Greek yogurt will work in this recipe—nonfat, low-fat, or full-fat. Choose your toppings, too. It's your kitchen, so it's your call.

· ◆ ·

1. Preheat the air fryer to 350°F.

2. In a large bowl, stir together the flour, sugar, baking powder, and salt. Add the yogurt and vanilla. With a wooden spoon, mix the dough until it is shaggy, and then knead it in the bowl until it holds together in a ball.

3. Divide the dough into 4 equal pieces. On a lightly floured work surface, roll each piece into a ball and pat into a disk about ½-inch thick. Poke your finger through the center of each disk to form into a doughnut shape. Spritz the doughnuts generously with canola oil.

4. Arrange the doughnuts in a single layer in the air fryer basket, with space between them. Air fry for 7 to 8 minutes, pausing halfway through the cooking time to flip the doughnuts, until golden brown.

5. To make the glaze: In a small bowl, mix together the sugar, butter, hot water, and vanilla until smooth. Stir in the food coloring (if using). When the doughnuts are cool enough to handle, dip them into the glaze and sprinkle on the accents (if using).

→ RUBY CHOCOLATE-GLAZED ←
CROISSANTS

MAKES
4 SERVINGS

PREP
5 MINUTES

TOTAL
20 MINUTES

1 (12-ounce) package frozen mini croissants

2 ounces ruby chocolate, coarsely chopped

2 teaspoons unsalted butter

¼ cup chopped pistachio meats

There's absolutely no shame in using a packaged product like plain frozen mini croissants to get a head start on a great dessert with your air fryer. Ruby chocolate is a gourmet chocolate with hints of berry flavors first introduced by the Belgian confectioner Barry Callebaut; if you can't find it easily, your favorite dark chocolate would work nicely here, too.

. . . . ◆ . . . .

1. Preheat the air fryer to 330°F.

2. Working in batches if necessary, arrange the croissants in a single layer in the air fryer basket about 2 inches apart. Air fry for 13 to 15 minutes, until golden brown and cooked through. Transfer to a cooling rack.

3. Meanwhile, in a small microwave-safe bowl, combine the chocolate and butter. Microwave on high in 30-second intervals, pausing to stir the chocolate, until melted and smooth.

4. When the croissants are cool enough to handle, dip the top side of the croissants into the chocolate sauce and scatter the pistachios on top. Serve warm.

→ AIR-FRIED ←
OREOS

MAKES
4 SERVINGS

PREP
10 MINUTES

TOTAL
20 MINUTES

1 (8-ounce) package crescent rolls

8 Oreo cookies

2 tablespoons powdered sugar

This treat is so incredibly simple to make with an air fryer, it almost doesn't require a recipe. However, given how popular deep-fried Oreos have become, they need a shout-out in these pages. Plus, you now have the perfect air fryer process and timing tested for you, so you can spend your time exploring the wide variety of Oreo flavors available.

. . . . •• ◆ •• . . . .

1. Preheat the air fryer to 350°F.

2. Unroll the crescent roll dough on a piece of parchment paper and pinch the seams together. Cut into 8 squares.

3. Place a cookie in the middle of each square and fold all the sides around the cookie. Pinch the seams to seal the dough around the cookie.

4. Arrange the cookies, seam-side down, in a single layer in the air fryer basket. Air fry for 8 minutes, pausing halfway through the cooking time to flip the cookies, until golden brown.

5. Sprinkle with the powdered sugar before serving.

→ AIR-FRIED ←
CANDY BARS

MAKES
4 SERVINGS

PREP
10 MINUTES

TOTAL
20 MINUTES

1 (8-ounce) package
crescent rolls

8 small "fun-size" candy bars,
such as Snickers or Milky Way

2 tablespoons
powdered sugar

Chocolate syrup (optional)

Whipped cream (optional)

Whoever first thought to batter-dip and deep-fry a candy bar was probably a genius. However, this air fryer version is pretty smart on its own merits because all it requires is a package of crescent rolls to transform your favorite candy into a sweet, unforgettable bundle of joy. Dress it up with a little chocolate syrup and a shot of whipped cream from a can and you will have created the embodiment of happiness on a plate.

· ◆ ·

1. Preheat the air fryer to 350°F.

2. Unroll the crescent roll dough on a piece of parchment paper and separate into 8 pieces.

3. Place a candy bar in the center of each piece and fold the wide edge of each roll over the candy; continue rolling as if making plain crescent rolls. To finish, roll each piece between your hands to ensure that the dough completely encloses the candy. Spritz generously with canola oil.

4. Arrange the pieces in a single layer in the air fryer basket, ensuring they do not touch. Air fry for 8 to 10 minutes, until golden brown.

5. Remove from the air fryer and let cool slightly. Dust with the powdered sugar. Serve drizzled with the chocolate syrup and whipped cream on the side (if using).

PEANUT BUTTER-MARSHMALLOW
DESSERT DIP

MAKES
4 SERVINGS

PREP
10 MINUTES

TOTAL
30 MINUTES

12 ounces mini peanut butter cups

12 ounces large marshmallows

12 graham crackers

Have you had a s'more recently? Those gooey, chocolaty, oh-so-good campfire treats are guaranteed to make you feel like a kid again. This easy air fryer recipe captures the taste indoors with less mess. Mini peanut butter cups are melted beneath a layer of marshmallows for a perfectly sweet and scoopable party dessert. The key is to use a baking dish that will fit in your air fryer, so adjust this recipe accordingly (you can always make another batch). If you have a cast-iron baking dish that fits, all the better.

1. Preheat the air fryer to 350°F.

2. Arrange the peanut butter cups in an even layer on the bottom of a baking dish that will fit your air fryer. Add the marshmallows in a single layer on top.

3. Place the dish in the air fryer basket and air fry for 15 to 20 minutes, until the marshmallows are golden and the chocolate is melted.

4. Serve warm with graham crackers for dipping.

→ ·CINNAMON-SUGAR·←
CHURROS

·MAKES·
8 SERVINGS

·PREP·
20 MINUTES

·TOTAL·
30 MINUTES +
REFRIGERATION TIME

½ cup + 2 tablespoons
sugar, divided

½ teaspoon ground cinnamon

1 cup water

5 tablespoons butter,
cut into 3 or 4 pieces

¼ teaspoon salt

1 cup all-purpose flour

2 large eggs

1 teaspoon vanilla extract

½ cup sweetened hazelnut
cocoa spread, such as Nutella

Refrigerating the churros before air frying is an essential step in this recipe, but keep it to about an hour or else they will begin to dry out. If you don't happen to have a piping bag, a freezer bag works pretty well. Just snip a small corner of the bag and place your tip attachment in the hole.

. . . . ◆ . . . .

1. In a small bowl, combine ½ cup of sugar and the cinnamon; mix until thoroughly combined, and set aside.

2. In a medium saucepan, add the water, butter, remaining 2 tablespoons of sugar, and salt. Bring to a boil over medium-high heat.

3. Reduce the heat to medium-low and add the flour. Stirring constantly with a rubber spatula, cook for about 2 minutes, until the dough is smooth. Remove from the heat and transfer the dough to a mixing bowl. Let cool for 5 minutes, then add the eggs and vanilla.

4. Using an electric mixer, mix until the dough comes together and resembles gluey mashed potatoes. Transfer the dough to a large piping bag fitted with a large star-shaped tip.

5. On a baking sheet lined with parchment paper, pipe the churros in 4-inch lengths and cut the ends with scissors. Sprinkle the churros with the cinnamon-sugar mixture and refrigerate for 1 hour.

6. Preheat the air fryer to 375°F.

7. Working in batches, use a spatula to carefully transfer the churros to the air fryer basket, arranging them in a single layer with about ½-inch space between them. Spritz generously with cooking oil spray. Air fry for 10 to 12 minutes, until golden brown.

8. Meanwhile, place the hazelnut cocoa spread in a microwave-safe dish. Heat on high for about a minute, pausing every 20 seconds to stir the sauce, until warm. Serve the churros warm with the spread for dipping on the side.

→ THE ULTIMATE NUTTY ←
BROWNIE SUNDAE

MAKES
2 SERVINGS

PREP
15 MINUTES

TOTAL
35 MINUTES +
COOLING TIME

¼ cup unsalted butter

3 ounces bittersweet chocolate, chopped (about ⅔ cup)

1 large egg

3 tablespoons granulated sugar

3 tablespoons light brown sugar

1½ teaspoons instant espresso granules

½ teaspoon vanilla extract

⅓ cup all-purpose flour

¼ cup chopped walnuts

⅛ teaspoon kosher salt

½ cup prepared caramel sauce, warmed

Pinch of flaky sea salt

1 cup vanilla ice cream

If you're looking for picture-perfect results with this dessert, you'll need to let your brownies cool completely and refrigerate them, preferably overnight, before cutting them to get perfectly clean edges. A few seconds in the microwave will warm them up again nicely. But then again, odds are you might want to dive right in after these are out of the air fryer.

. . . . ◆ . . . .

1. Preheat the air fryer to 300°F.

2. Grease and flour a 5 x 7-inch (3-cup) glass baking dish. Set aside.

3. In a large microwave-safe bowl, combine the butter and chocolate. Microwave on high in 30-second increments, pausing to stir, until melted and smooth, about 90 seconds total. Let cool slightly, about 10 minutes.

4. Add the egg, granulated sugar, brown sugar, espresso granules, and vanilla to the cooled butter-chocolate mixture and whisk until well combined. Add the flour, walnuts, and kosher salt; stir until combined. Pour the batter evenly into the prepared baking dish.

5. Place the dish in the air fryer basket. Air fry for about 18 to 20 minutes, until the top and sides are set and a toothpick inserted into the center comes out with some moist clumps attached.

6. Let cool about 15 minutes. Serve drizzled with the caramel sauce, sprinkled with the sea salt, and topped with vanilla ice cream.

→ SWEET ←
MAPLE-BACON TWISTS

MAKES
4 SERVINGS

PREP
15 MINUTES

TOTAL
30 MINUTES

2 tablespoons pure maple syrup

½ teaspoon cayenne (optional)

¼ teaspoon salt

1 (12-ounce) package reduced-sodium, center-cut bacon

3 tablespoons brown sugar, divided

Bacon for dessert? Why not? These sweet treats are so easy to prepare in an air fryer and are guaranteed to charm your favorite bacon fans. If you don't enjoy this meat candy on its own, use it as a garnish on a fancy apple pie, or chop it up and scatter it over a peanut butter ice cream sundae. It also fits well as part of a fruit and cheese platter.

. . . . ◆ . . . .

1. Preheat the air fryer to 400°F.

2. In a small bowl, combine the syrup, cayenne (if using), and salt; stir until thoroughly combined.

3. Working one piece at a time, lay the bacon flat on a piece of parchment paper and brush both sides with the syrup mixture. Starting at one end, twist the bacon into a long, tight spiral and place in the air fryer basket. Repeat until all of the bacon is in the basket, arranged in a single layer (it is fine if the pieces touch one another).

4. Scatter half of the brown sugar over the bacon and air fry for about 15 minutes, pausing halfway through the cooking time to flip the bacon and scatter with the remaining sugar.

5. Let the bacon sit in the air fryer basket until it is cool enough to handle.

→ SALTED CHOCOLATE ←
OATMEAL COOKIES

MAKES
13 COOKIES

PREP
15 MINUTES

TOTAL
30 MINUTES

½ cup unsalted butter, at room temperature

½ cup brown sugar, lightly packed

¼ cup granulated sugar

1 teaspoon vanilla extract

2 large eggs

1 cup all-purpose flour

¾ cup old-fashioned oats

½ teaspoon baking soda

½ teaspoon kosher salt

6 ounces dark chocolate, chopped into chunks

¼ cup raisins or dried cranberries (optional)

¼ cup walnuts or pecans, chopped (optional)

Sea salt

Cookies now or later? It's your choice! This cookie dough freezes beautifully, so you can keep a batch tucked away until the cookie urge hits. A few minutes later, you're in chocolate heaven with something that tastes like it's fresh from your favorite gourmet cookie shop. If you go this route, shape into individual balls before freezing, add a few extra minutes to the air fryer time, and sprinkle with the sea salt just after the cookies are out of the air fryer.

. . . . ◆ . . . .

1. Preheat the air fryer to 375°F. Cut a piece of parchment paper to fit in the bottom of the air fryer basket and set it on your work surface.

2. In a large bowl, combine the butter and sugar; use an electric mixer to beat until light and fluffy, about 3 minutes. Add the vanilla and eggs and beat again until thoroughly combined. Add the flour, oats, baking soda, and salt and mix again just until thoroughly combined. Use a silicone spatula to stir in the chocolate. Add in the dried fruit and nuts (if using).

3. Working in batches, use two spoons to scoop round balls of dough and place in the air fryer basket about 2 inches apart. Top each cookie with a small pinch of sea salt. Air fry for 10 to 12 minutes, until browned. Carefully transfer the cookies to a baking rack and let cool completely before serving.

INDEX